Sonny

Ron Gabriel

iUniverse, Inc.
Bloomington

Sonny

Copyright © 2012 by Ron Gabriel.

All rights reserved. No part of this book may be used or reproduced by any means, graphic, electronic, or mechanical, including photocopying, recording, taping or by any information storage retrieval system without the written permission of the publisher except in the case of brief quotations embodied in critical articles and reviews.

iUniverse books may be ordered through booksellers or by contacting:

iUniverse
1663 Liberty Drive
Bloomington, IN 47403
www.iuniverse.com
1-800-Authors (1-800-288-4677)

Because of the dynamic nature of the Internet, any web addresses or links contained in this book may have changed since publication and may no longer be valid. The views expressed in this work are solely those of the author and do not necessarily reflect the views of the publisher, and the publisher hereby disclaims any responsibility for them.

Any people depicted in stock imagery provided by Thinkstock are models, and such images are being used for illustrative purposes only.
Certain stock imagery © Thinkstock.

ISBN: 978-1-4759-4859-2 (sc)
ISBN: 978-1-4759-4858-5 (hc)
ISBN: 978-1-4759-4857-8 (ebk)

Library of Congress Control Number: 2012917494

Printed in the United States of America

iUniverse rev. date: 09/25/2012

Sonny

This book is lovingly dedicated to Ester Maxine Owens, my Aunt Max. She did so much for me and my whole extended family. The example she set in the sharing and giving way she lived her life was her admirable legacy. Her presence in my life had such a positive effect. She was, in fact, my second mother. How fortunate I was to have had two such inspirational women in my life.

CONTENTS

ACKNOWLEDGMENT

I want to thank my wonderful wife for putting up with me yelling for her to spell a word for me. The computer has a helpful spell check program, but the way I spell, sometimes I get a, *no suggestion*. This reply is the computers way of saying, "You're waaay off, what a dummy you are." When I get this answer, I yell for my wife, "Joyce how do you spell—?" She has yelled back for over ten years as I have birthed these stories of my life. She has saved me many times from the *demon* computer's anger.

My computer has a personality all it's own. Some days it's feeling good and we get along perfectly. Then other days it turns on me with a vengeance, like an angry caged tiger attacking it's trainer. I really don't know what gets into it; the computer takes it's good old time booting up, it won't spell right and it hides files. It also goes so far as to delete e-mails that I wanted to keep. *What did I do*? Maybe I hurt it's feelings. Can you hurt a computer's feelings?

But I am digressing. My wife helped me edit all these vague story ideas into an organized readable copy. She also has listened to my endless chatter about my wannabe book project.

Special thanks also has to go to Kay Conklin and Phil Dunham for their help, support and positive encouragement over the many years of our long friendship.

Ron Gabriel
2012

INTRODUCTION

There comes a point in life when you realize that you are closer to the end than the beginning. Some people go into denial, some try not to think about it, while others throw themselves into the present day with a vengeance. I wrote a book.

I was born and raised in a small town in central Ohio named Delaware. This small town is noted for being the birthplace of Rutherford B. Hayes, the nineteenth president of the United States. Ohio Wesleyan University is located in Delaware and The Little Brown Jug harness race is held here every fall during the Delaware County Fair.

Some of the stories in this book took place as I grew up east of the river in the 1940s and early 1950s. I lived in a blue-collar neighborhood full of kids. We were on our own to run free in the empty lots, back yards and along the banks of the Olentangy River.

My nickname in the old neighborhood was, "Sonny." It has been well over six decades since I have been called by that name. Writing these memories has afforded me the pleasure of rummaging through that time of my life.

The experiences I had and the people I knew in that era help mold me into the person I am today. I am sharing these stories of that time, which are slowly fading away into the forgotten past. My hope is to document what once was.

I have also taken the liberty to comment on some current issues of the day. These ramblings are meant to give the reader a humorous perspective on my life and times.

Come along with Sonny in his journey through life.

THE BEGINNING

It was a clear, mild Friday night for March 29, 1935, in Delaware, Ohio. Marie Owens Gabriel would not be going to the Strand Theater to see *Charlie Chan Goes to Paris*. She was in Jane M. Case Hospital delivering a son at 10:32 pm with the help of Doctor Arnold and her husband Finley Morse Gabriel. The son was named Ronald Morse Gabriel.

The new parents brought their son home to a rented 1½-story house at 232 West William Street. On the birth certificate, the mother was listed as a housewife and the father was listed as a mechanic for Northern Ohio Telephone Company.

When my sister, Sally, was born eighteen months earlier, mother promptly went to bed for a month. She figured she had the baby so it was up to someone else to take care of it. Dad and mom's sisters were first in line for care duty. The story goes that Dad came home from work and Aunt Monnie and Aunt Maxine (mom's sisters) were arguing as to who was in charge. Dad, who didn't like conflict, chose Aunt Max because she was a nurse.

Both of my parents were raised on farms. Dad was one of thirteen and in mom's family there were nine. I never heard them telling stories of the good old days on the farm. I got the impression that life on the farm was long hours and hard work. I surmise that Sally and I were the first babies born in a hospital in many generations.

In 1935, the country was coming out of the *Great Depression*. Franklin D. Roosevelt was president when Social Security started in 1935; a gallon of gas was a dime, a loaf of bread was eight cents, the average yearly wage was $1,600.00 and the unemployment rate was 20.1%.

At that time, in Delaware, many people had an icebox; a wood/coal stove that did not heat the upstairs; milk delivered in bottles to the door by a horse-drawn wagon; and an outhouse.

The last of the *Greatest Generation* was born in 1927, so they made it into World War II. From 1928 to 1944 was my generation, which was called the *Silent Generation*. Not many people know it even existed. In 1945, the *Baby Boomers* blasted onto the scene sired by the *Greatest Generation*.

LIFE ON THE FARM

My earliest memories are of living on the farm, State Route 37, five miles west of Delaware, where mom and her sisters and brothers grew up. The arrangement was that mom and dad would take care of my grandmother, who suffered from dementia, for free rent. The only memory I have of her is that she sat and stared vacantly into space most of the time.

The farm was a wonderful place for a small kid. We had chickens, sheep, hogs, horses, rats in the corn crib and a black and white mixed border collie named Major. A family lived down the road that had a girl my sister's age and a boy my age. We had a big barn to play in that had a haymow. This was before they baled hay so we had all that loose hay to jump around on and tunnel in. The boy from down the road and I would play for hours in a dirt pile, making imaginary highways and parking lots for our toy trucks and cars. Mom would bring out huge pieces of bread with homemade apple butter on top for a treat.

It was the late 1930s, so electric, telephone, and inside plumbing had not yet reached the farm. I remember the old coal oil lamp that was our only source of light at night. We had a wood/coal stove in the middle of the living room that tried to heat the house. When it was really cold, we pulled the couch and chairs up next to the stove to keep warm. The old windows let a lot of cold air in on windy days. The wind would sometimes blow down the stovepipe and pop open the stove door and dark, gritty soot would spread through the room. The first thing I remember hearing each morning was Dad banging the poker on the inside of the stove, starting up the smoldering embers to rekindle the fire for the day. In the summer, dad would dismantle the stove and take it to the barn.

There was a big water trough between the barnyard and the drive which supplied water for the farm animals. One evening my sister and I were standing there when the neighbor watered the big plow horses after a long day in the fields. One of the horses reared up on its back legs. To me the horse seemed fifty feet tall; it startled and scared me. I think the neighbor did it as a prank but it changed, forever, my feelings toward horses. I was once also flopped by a big rooster; but the real villain of the farm was the buck sheep. Bucks are mean by nature but this one took pride in his meanness. My sister and I would hide in the upstairs closet and wonder if the buck could climb the stairs.

There were many wonderful days of adventure on the farm. We could play down by the creek and throw cow pies at each other. Yes, cow pies are exactly what you think they are. We could play hide-and-go-seek in the barn or swing on the big hay ropes and drop into the soft hay. The higher you jumped from, the higher you would bounce. It's a wonder we didn't break our necks. When it rained, water would rise in the ditch in front of the house next to the road and mom would let us play in it like our own private pool.

I can't remember gathering eggs; they probably didn't trust me to not break them because we needed them for food. I do remember helping mom catch the chickens to ring their necks, pluck the feathers, and then feed fried chicken to the company that always came on Sunday. We always had a lot of company; aunts, uncles, cousins, neighbors and dad's drinking buddies.

My dog, Major, at least I remember him as my dog, was at my side all day. He would go out and prowl at night and he loved to fight other dogs and make puppies. Some mornings he would come back in pretty bad shape. A little game I played with him was to wait until he was looking the other way, then I would take off running as fast as I could and try to lose him. He would turn, spot me and lope over and catch me quite easily. I never won that game. It didn't take much for us to enjoy ourselves on the farm.

Life was good but grandmother died and my uncle, who had inherited the farm, decided we had to move. I was going to be six so it was time to start school. Mom and dad wanted me to go to sight-saving school in Columbus, Ohio. I had worn glasses since I was two. We moved to the eastside of Delaware on Flax Street. We couldn't take Major because he got in too many dogfights so he stayed on the farm with my uncle.

STARTING SCHOOL

One of the most traumatic times of my life was going to sight-saving school in Columbus, Ohio, for the first and second grades. We had just moved from the simple, quiet life on the farm to small town life in Delaware and then I started school in the very big city of Columbus. The week before my first day of school, I became aware that something big was going to happen and it made me fearful. The first day of school, Aunt Ruth (not an aunt) came over in her car. We all got in and drove to Columbus. We pulled up in front of Fairview Elementary School and mom and I went in. I was introduced to Mrs. Orball, my teacher. I held onto mom for dear life. Finally they tore me away while I was crying and sat me down at my new desk. The first project of school was putting little beads on a string. I accidentally spilled the beads all over the floor. *Welcome to the first grade.*

I rode the Greyhound bus from Delaware early on Monday mornings to Columbus and came back after school on Fridays. There were three other boys from Delaware who did the same thing. We stayed with a private family for the week. She was a nice person but her husband wanted nothing to do with us. We would listen to the Lone Ranger on the radio after supper at 6:30 and then it was off to bed. I was a bed-wetter so I wasn't allowed any water at supper or after but I would suck water out of my toothbrush on the sly.

I attended Fairview School for two years. I failed the second grade. Mom told me later that I received all S's (satisfactory) the first half and all U's (unsatisfactory) the second half. She also said that I would wake up in the night asking if it was time to leave for Columbus. I can remember dad walking me to the bus station on dark cold mornings in the winter. The snow would crunch under our feet and I would try and step where dad had stepped in the heavy snow.

I don't think the sight-saving program helped me much. I was in a regular school with other regular kids. The only thing they taught us was to place a piece of cardboard under the line we were reading so our eyes could focus on the line better. Mom decided to pull me out of sight-saving school and put me in the local public school for which she received much opposition from her family and the school system. She also decided that I would take the second grade over again. Failing the second grade made me feel ashamed and self-conscious; that summer I had to tell all the other kids in the neighborhood that I flunked. Also, all my life, I have been ashamed to tell people that I had to go to sight-saving school. Later, in high school, if the subject came up of why I was older than the other kids in my class I would jokingly say, "My second grade teacher liked me so much, she wanted to keep me for another year."

I think my parents felt sight-saving school would help me; but I felt that I had no alterative and should not show or say anything against it. My reaction was just to bury it and not think about it. Putting it into perspective now many kids have had much worse experiences. I had caring parents who made many sacrifices to provide a stable home life for me.

EAST SCHOOL

I started the second grade at East School in Delaware, Ohio. The year was 1943. East School was a two-story brick building built in 1913. The playground circled the school building and was bordered by three streets and an alley. The boys and girls were separated, each having their own playground at recess. There were four grade schools in Delaware. North School was the top of the social economic heap followed by West School. East School was in a blue-collar area and our dad's carried black lunchboxes to work. South School was predominately colored, the term for African Americans at that time.

My first couple of days at school were intimidating. I had been given all the vaccination shots and they "really took." My arms were swollen down past the elbows and were so sore that my sister had her latest beau, Hank Spencer, watch out for me. I would wait until all the other kids left the room so I wouldn't get jostled.

The teachers at East School were there for a generation or two and taught the same grades for over twenty years. The books were passed out the first day of school. At that time books lasted for many years.

There would be a list of names on the inside cover of the kids that had the book in previous years. It was exciting to see who had signed the inside cover, thus knowing who's book you were going to use this year.

Our wooden desks had tops that folded up so we could store our books and pencils inside. The top to the desk had about a two inch size hole that used to be an ink well. The desks were lined up in rows facing the teacher and were never moved. Large, dark pictures of George Washington and Abraham Lincoln hung on the wall while a well-worn American flag stood in the corner. Blackboards covered two walls with windows on the other wall. At the back of the room was a coatroom with hooks to hang up our coats. A partition separated the classroom from the coatroom with an opening at each end.

I always sat in the front row so I could see the blackboard. The teacher had a big, wooden desk facing the students. The first thing we did each morning was to say the *Pledge of Allegiance* to the flag. The first year we extended our arm out shoulder high with the palm of our hand up as we said the *Pledge*. The next year someone had decided that this gesture was too close to the Heil Hitler sign so we stopped.

East school was six blocks from home. We walked both ways as well as coming home for lunch. It was only up hill one way.

We had a class bully named Pudge Ward, also known as Harry Brown. When he died years later, the paper said his real name was Harry Bryant. He wasn't real mean but you knew who was boss on the play ground. Don Boring was the only kid that would stand up to Pudge. I think Pudge, or Harry, bluffed a lot and really wanted to be liked under that tough attitude.

It seemed to me the preferred recess activity was a fistfight. If there wasn't one going on, the boys were trying to get one started. I wore glasses and worried about getting them broken. I hated the name four-eyes or specks. I didn't belong to any particular gang. I just sort of watched things, not unlike looking at a movie, although I didn't feel like I was alone or a loaner.

Mr. Conger was the principal and also taught the sixth grade. He was a tall man with a paunch and wore a suit and tie every day. He ran the school with strictness and all the boys were afraid of his paddle. He would tell stories and we would have to figure out the hidden meaning. In the spring, he would read a poem that started "Barefoot boy, cheeks of tan, rolled up pantaloons." Then he would tell the boys that he wanted to see some of us come to school barefooted the next day. We gladly complied.

When I look back on my five years at East School, it was a great time for me. It was the war years and the home front spent its time just waiting and doing whatever we could to help. Kids tried to do their part and saved dimes, aluminum foil, and picked milkweed pods. I heard that the pods were used in the making of life jackets. Then one day a note was brought into my third grade class to Mrs. Chriswell. She looked up and told us the war in Europe was over and she started to cry. She said, "I knew those Germans would have to surrender."

Things started to change in the sixth grade; I got a paper route, which exposed me to other areas of town and the kids who lived in those areas. The war was finally over and we were looking forward to going to Willis High School for the next six years. The word was that the north and west side kids looked down on us "eastsiders," but frankly I never experienced any of that. I wasn't sure about leaving the comfort of East School, but knew I was being propelled into a new life. I had no idea of all the exciting experiences and new friends that awaited me at the next level.

SUMMER

In reminiscing about childhood, two days stand out for me: Christmas Day and the day school let out for the summer. The last day of school was always special. We were allowed to bring a guest, either a little brother, sister or some younger buddy from the neighborhood. After the final bell, we headed out the door. The summer was before us! A great feeling of joy and freedom would come over me, like having a big birthday cake put in front of you with three months' worth of servings.

Summer was the time to go barefoot and to meet the gang in the empty lot down the street that we used for a ball field or meeting place. Summer was for climbing trees, raiding the neighbor's apple tree, playing cowboys and Indians or war. It was the time to explore down by the river or fish with a stick and string. One of the kids had a rope, with a knot at the end, hanging from the limb of a tall tree and we would play for hours taking turns flying through the air over make believe rivers, escaping like Tarzan from the villains of the jungle.

Sometimes we would find a grape-arbor and pick the hard little unripe grapes for our homemade slingshots. We also made bow and arrows from small tree limbs. We would build a fort from old boards and pretend that we were protecting the neighborhood from Indians. In the evening, we would play tag in the street while our parents watched from their porches. On rare occasions, we would beg for a nickel from our parents and go for an ice cream cone.

No matter what game we were playing or what adventure we were acting out, all of us came running when the iceman drove up in his truck. We would wait until he hoisted the heavy ice block on his padded shoulder and disappear into the house. We would then dash to the rear bumper of the ice truck, hurriedly pull back the canvas, scoop up the ice slivers and pop them in our mouths. Oh how cool and refreshing they tasted!

A quick retreat was made before he came back. I never knew whether he cared if we had ice slivers or not, but it was another fun summer adventure.

Most of the summer activities would take place within calling distance of our moms. If we wanted to do something special, like going two or three blocks from home, we had to get permission.

Sometime around the middle of August, mom would call me in and we would go downtown to buy school clothes and supplies. Then I knew my summer days of freedom and playing were numbered. The school bell would soon ring, calling me back. I would try to play a little harder and stay up later to fight off the coming of Labor Day and school. But on the first Tuesday after the first Monday in September, mom would get me up and I would put on my new jeans and clodhoppers. (A heavy, above the ankle shoe with a thick sole.} Then she would run a damp comb through my unruly hair, kiss me and send me off to school. Summer was over.

THE OLD NEIGHBORHOOD

I grew up on the east side of Delaware in the early forties. In a three-square block area, there were probably twenty-five kids. In those days, the kids had nicknames like Buddy, Sis, Pudge, Lefty, Butch and mine was Sonny. I asked my dad once why they called me Sonny. He said, "Because you are so bright, we have to put you under the bathtub to tell when the sun comes up." That sounded good to me.

In our neighborhood there were so many characters both old and young that I hardly know where to begin. There was Mrs. Spencer who walked with a great limp because one leg was much shorter than the other due to a poorly set broken leg when she was young. When she would get mad at her husband, which was often, she would pound loudly on the piano and sing old church hymns at the top of her lungs. There was Charlie Wright. When he got a snoot full, he would throw back his head and give out with one of those special yells that was full of the sheer joy of life. He would also eat raw eggs by cracking them over his mouth and letting the egg drop in; as kids we were impressed and liked to watch him do that feat. Mr. Welch had two nice apple trees that we would raid. Mrs. Skates had the loudest voice in the neighborhood. When she called Shirley and Ginger, you could hear her for blocks.

In those days, everyone's windows and doors had screens that were open during the summer, thus letting the sounds of the neighborhood drift through the air. We could hear family arguments or kids laughing and playing. If your nose was good enough, you might be able to smell what was for supper across the street. There were no secrets in the old neighborhood.

Part of the adventure and prestige of the neighborhood was it's close proximity to the Olentangy River. When you live next to a river, there is never a dull day. We could fish, explore the banks for turtles or snakes or see who could skip a flat stone across the water the most times.

Some of my most vivid memories were the summer evenings after supper. The grownups would set on their front porches and yell to each other across the street as we played games like, "Ollie, Ollie, in-free," with the telephone pole as base. One of the kids would count to one hundred by fives with their eyes covered. He or she would then try to find the other kids that were hiding. After awhile, if everyone hadn't been found, the one that counted would yell, "Ollie, Ollie in-free; all that's out can come in free."

As the dark would catch us playing in the street and yards, the mothers would start their melodious chant:

> "Buddy, where are you?"
> "Sis, you have to come in now."
> "Butch, it's getting dark."
> "Sonny, it's time for bed."

The neighborhood would soon get quiet. The last sounds of the day would drift in my open bedroom window as I lay in bed; Mr. Spencer's car headed for Lake Street, Charlie and Thelma coming home from the movie, the muffled sounds on the radio drifting up the stairway to my bedroom or the lonesome sound of the train whistle echoing through the summer evening. Then mom would say, "Sonny, get to sleep."

CHOOSING UP SIDES

I never liked choosing up sides when I was a kid. I was never chosen first. It was closer to last or even last.

The way it worked was, we would meet in someone's back yard or an empty lot, which we confiscated as our own ball field. Then we would decide to play a game. Two of the gang would be captains. I never knew how you got to be a captain. It was probably a self-appointed position. The captains then took turns choosing who would be on their team. The rest of us just stood there waiting and hoping that we would be chosen early. It always came down to the most unathletic or small kids that were chosen last. Since I wore glasses it reduced my potential in this draft.

If we played baseball and you were put in right field, that was not a good sign. If we played football and you were put on the line so that you didn't get to touch the ball, that also was not a good sign. If we played basketball and no one passed you the ball, that too, was a very bad sign.

We all enjoyed having pickup games. We were just on our own so the choosing up sides was the worst part but it only lasted for a short time. Once the game began, we were our own referees and umpires and we made up our own rules. A lot of time was taken up by disputes as to where the ball hit, was someone off sides, or if there had been a foul ball. Sometimes these discussions could not be settled. In most cases it boiled down to whose ball it was or who was the biggest of the arguers.

Games were often called for various reasons:

> Because the boy who owned the ball was called home by his mother,
> people that owned the yard asked us to leave,

the baseball broke a window; that was the quickest way to clear the field,
some girls walked up and wanted to play,
a smaller kid got hurt,
or we just got tired of arguing so decided to do something else.

The bottom line was that we were kids out entertaining ourselves, enjoying sports in the great outdoors, like kids are supposed to do.

CLIMBING TREES

Can you remember, when you were a kid, how much fun it was to climb a tree? A tree was meant to be climbed, like a puddle was meant to be walked through and a retaining stone wall was meant to be walked on.

Climbing a tree was a happy carefree expression of youth just like the freedom of running through the grass barefooted. Trees were our friends. We hung out in them and talked or came to them for apples, peaches or cherries. I remember the cry in the old neighborhood, "Mr. Welch's apple tree has apples!" and we all ran gleefully there. My first smoke was corncob silk, rolled up in newspaper strips, under Mr. Welch's apple tree. Ah, the good old days, a tree and a good smoke, what more could a kid want.

No one in our neighborhood had a tree house. That was a kid's ultimate dream: to have a tree house that could be used as a secret clubhouse. We did have a clubhouse for a while down the alley. It was in an old shed that was locked so we couldn't get in. We had to crawl on our bellies under the locked door. It is remarkable how small a space a kid can squeeze through. It smelled dank, had a dirt floor and cobwebs hanging down, but it was a cool place to us. It was a secret place our parents didn't know about. We were on our own and could do anything we wanted.

Let's see, what did we do? Most of our energies were spent rounding up the gang and crawling into the clubhouse without being seen and I am sure we used swear words just to let our buddies know that we knew them.

The old clubhouse came to an end when a few of the gang decided it would be fun to set off some dynamite caps. Joey McIntire came in just in time to throw a board and himself on the caps. He got hurt and went to the hospital, which was a big deal at that time. He was the only kid from the neighborhood that I knew that went to the hospital. Mom sent me over to see him when he came home. I stood by his bed and didn't know what to say. He had big white bandages all over him and he was in real pain. Joey carried those marks on his body the rest of his life but he may have saved the lives of the kids who were in the clubhouse that day.

I miss the joy of climbing trees. The higher you climb, the better the view. Climbing was a retreat from reality. You could pretend that you were in the jungle with Tarzan or in a high bell tower where no one could see you. But my climbing days are over. I could still walk through the grass barefooted but I haven't done it in years. I wonder if kids of today climb trees? If not, they're missing a memorable part of growing up.

THE SEARS AND ROEBUCK ORDER

As a youngster, I had a buddy named Junior. He lived down the alley from me, along the river. His house was a small one-story frame whose rooms had been added on one at a time. I liked to visit him because his family liked to laugh and joke a lot. They had a type of humor I didn't hear at home.

Christmas was coming and Junior and I were beginning to make our Christmas wish list.

Junior's parents said they had a big order at Sears and Roebuck for Christmas and it was due in any day. By this time in our young lives, we had heard at school that there was no Santa, which was crushing news. Neither of us had a fireplace for Santa to slide down. We knew that it wouldn't be safe for Santa's sleigh to land on our roof, so we had early suspicions.

Junior and I would mention something we wanted and his Mother would think for a minute and then give us a smile and say, "You know, I think that just might be in the Sears order."

It was getting close to Christmas and the order still hadn't come in. I began to worry for them, so I asked Junior's father, "What are you going to do if the order doesn't get here in time?" He replied, "We will just have to go and buy some small presents to make do."

A couple of days before Christmas, Junior and I went to the Saturday afternoon movie. On the way home I said to Junior, "Lets hurry because maybe the Sears and Roebuck order is in." He turned to me and said, "There is no order. My parents are just saying that because there's no money for Christmas." I was dumbfounded. I didn't know what to say. They sure fooled me.

I think of that story sometimes when we have a big Christmas with lots of presents under the tree. Not everybody is as fortunate as I have been.

SLEDDING

Back in the 1940s, when Delaware got a heavy snow, the city closed down Liberty Street hill, from University to William Street. Kids from all over town flocked there to sled. I can only remember sledding at night. The sleds were wooden with metal frames. It was cold and the word was, "Don't put your tongue on the metal frame. Your tongue will stick to it." That was more of a challenge than a warning. Well, they were right; your tongue did stick to it. It was painful to pull off and you learned your lesson with one lick.

The city also closed Franklin Street hill. It was a steeper hill that ran from University Street to Spring then William. Don't look for this hill any more; it has been covered up with a new Wesleyan building. Wesleyan had three more sled hills; Styvansant Hall had two hills, one in front on William Street and one in back. The 3rd was down by the old sulfur springs, which is also gone. I saw my first set of skis used on that hill by George Crowl.

We had our own hill on the east side. It was on Flax Street and ran from Grace down past Milo Street and on past the old Chair Factory until the sled stopped. It wasn't as busy as the other hills. It was not officially closed by the city. In that era there was much less traffic. The local drivers knew not to use Flax Street when it snowed. It was close to home and all the old neighborhood gang was there.

Harry Bardgill used to bring this long, homemade, wooden toboggan that about seven kids could fit on. One of my great feats in grade school was, while using my own sled, I caught up with *The Toboggan* and jumped from my sled onto Harry's toboggan, leaving my sled to drift off to the side. Then I rode the rest of the way in style on the chariot of wood. On a cold winter evening, with the old gang watching, it was an event legends are made of.

Another time I made a famous run on the sidewalk from the top of E. Central Avenue hill. It started at the Mobile filling station at the corner of Lake Street and ran down across Grace and Milo Streets ending triumphantly in front of Virginia Smith's house next to the Olentangy River. I was on my way home from school, with sled in tow, when that run spontaneously happened. There was no one there to confirm it, so it was never officially recognized.

It's been in the neighborhood of sixty-five years since I have used a sled, but I can still feel the encrusted snow on my winter mackinaw; my snowy, wet, cold, cold feet and see my breath vaporize into the winter evening. I can hear the joyful sounds of kids squealing and shouting and the crunch of the snow under my feet as I made the long walk back up the hill.

The evening ended when mom's voice drifted across the white snow, "Sonny it's time to come home. You have school tomorrow." Did you ever realize that when you were a kid, the last voice you heard at night and the first voice you heard in the morning was your mothers?

GABBY HAYES

The image of Gabby Hayes has been rolling around in my mind lately. My mind must not be focused on the great issues of the day.

Gabby was Roy Roger's sidekick. He was a bearded, scruffy cowboy who looked like he had been on the trail too long. He never got to kiss the girl but he did get to hold the horses, if that is any consolation. You know, come to think of it, Roy, Gene or Hoppy (Hopalong Cassidy) never got in any romances either. They were too busy hunting down the dirty varmints that rampaged through the old West.

Most of the movie cowboys wore two guns. They really looked cool but can you imagine carrying two guns around all day long. Think of the process of getting on a horse or setting in a chair to eat. No wonder all they did was stand at the bar and drink sarsaparilla.

When I was ten, they were my heroes. They roamed the west, having adventures, free of school and parents. Sometimes at the end of the movie, it looked like this was the time one of them was going to settle down with a girl he'd taken a fancy to. The other cowboys would say their goodbyes and head down the trail, thinking the old gang was finally breaking up. But by the time they got to the pass, they would hear a horse running hard to catch up. By golly, it was their old buddy who couldn't settle down after all. They would all have a big laugh and head down the trail, free as the wind.

When I watched the old westerns, I knew who the good guys were and who the bad guys were.

I also knew that the good guys always won, no exceptions. Of all the gunfights that Roy, Gene and Hoppy were in, they never took a bullet. That's phenomenal, not one. So why am I still thinking about Gabby Hayes? He was an icon of a bygone era. There are only a few of us left that remember him and his buddies that so thoroughly entertained us in our childhood. Gabby reminds me of all the Saturday afternoons that I begged sixteen cents from mom, jumped on my bike and rode downtown to the Strand Theater. There were always lots of kids making lots of noise. Usually, every kid you knew was there, so you were a part of a group that got three hours of fun and excitement for your sixteen cents.

TARZAN

Another one of my heroes about that time was Tarzan. He lived in a neat tree house and seemed carefree and happy swinging on vines from tree to tree traveling thru the jungle.

Tarzan had a pet monkey named Cheeta. Actually, all the animals in the jungle were his friends. All he had to do was use his "Tarzan call" to summon them. They would come running and help him if he was in trouble. Elephants helped Tarzan more than any other animal. Sometimes he would ride on them and tell them what to do with grunts and secret hand signals.

When moving through the jungle, from tree to tree, he could always swing down and surprise the scoundrels who were up to no good in the peaceful jungle. The bad guys usually spoke with an accent and used a monocle. One of the great perils of the jungle was quicksand. The villains didn't seem to know about quicksand and they paid the price. They would get stuck and someone would yell, "Don't struggle, it will pull you under!" But the man in the quicksand (it was never a woman) never listened. He would start thrashing around yelling for help. Then, slowly, down he would go, into the quicksand. Someone would get a stick and try to help him, but it would never work. The stick would break and all you would see is just a hand, a muffled scream and then nothing. Of course, just the bad guys died in the quicksand.

Jane joined Tarzan in his tree house. Tarzan didn't talk much, so "Me Tarzan, you Jane," was usually the longest line in the movie. After Jane, came Boy; now there were mouths to feed. Tarzan was resourceful so I didn't worry about that. I was never sure how Boy got there, but at ten, life was full of mysteries.

They all had a good time swimming in their private lagoon with a waterfall in the background. Once in a while, a crocodile would appear but Tarzan would swim over and wrestle it into submission. Of course, since he was a super swimmer, he swam in every movie. We used to tie a rope to a limb of a tall tree and pretend we were Tarzan swinging through the jungle. We would try and imitate the famous "Tarzan call," but I think all we did was scare the animals away rather then attract them. After all, there's only one Tarzan!

Interesting fact from the internet's Wikipedia: The Tarzan novels were written by American author Edgar Rice Burroughs; first appearing as stories in magazines in 1912 and novel form in 1914.

Johnny Weissmuller, the most well known of the actors who played Tarzan, won 5 Olympic Gold Medals, 52 National Swimming Championships and set 67 world records during the 1920s. He made 12 Tarzan movies during the 1930s and 1940s.

THE MONKEYS' HOLE

There was a mystic place of youth on the Olentangy River, north of the Central Avenue bridge, called, "The Monkeys' Hole." It was located where the old dam used to connect to the east bank.

The big square quarry stones lay haphazardly around the bank. Some big trees that floated down the river got lodged between the stones left over from the torn out dam. This created a "backwater" which made a pond that was away from the flow of the river. It became a swimming hole for the neighborhood. I don't know how it got its name but all of us kids called it The Monkeys' Hole.

Most of our parents forbid us to swim in the river. At that time it was believed you could catch polio from river water. But it was impossible to keep us away from the river, as it was close, free and a lot of fun at our age. It was an adventure somewhat like Tom Sawyer on the Mississippi. We even had an old rope that we attached to a tree on the bank so we could swing out and drop in the water.

I learned to swim there. I would run out on a fallen tree that served as a diving board and jump as far out in the water as I could. Joey McIntire, who was older, said he would jump in and bring me back to the bank. He did a couple of times, then must have gotten tired of pulling me in, so he yelled "Swim!" Then he yelled instructions to me on how to move my arms and legs. I got to going and triumphantly dog-paddled to the muddy bank.

One sunny day I was down by the river with my dog and I decided to take my clothes off and go for a swim. When I got out, the dog had carried away some of my clothes, including my shoes with my glasses in them. I tried to explain this to my parents but I still got a paddling for swimming in the river.

Dad always said before he switched me, "This is going to hurt me more than it does you." I could never figure that out so I asked him once about it. He started to say something, then he stopped, then he started again—stopped and finally ended up with, "You will understand when you get older."

The gang of boys in our neighborhood thought we owned the Monkeys' Hole, but Harry Spencer's gang from up around Bardgill's junkyard started using it too. They would come down Flax Street hill four abreast like an invading army. They acted like they didn't have to sneak because their parents didn't care if they swam in the river. Along about this time, I had a bike and a paper route. I could ride by myself up to the county pool at the Fairgrounds. I gave up the Old Monkey's Hole because I was getting tired of the consequences of swimming in the river.

In 1961 the Highway Department built a new four-lane bridge on Central Avenue. They channeled out the river to make it flow evenly. In doing so, the remnants of the old dam were removed and the banks were cleared of fallen trees and that was the end of the old Monkeys' Hole. By then we were grown up doing different things far from the muddy banks of the Olentangy River. The kids now-a-days are chauffeured to new chlorine filled, clean-water pools full of rope buoys and signs painted on the side telling the depth of the pool with capable lifeguards always on duty. Where's the adventure?

A PERFECT SUMMER DAY

I remember the great joy of jumping on my bike and heading for the Delaware County Swimming Pool, looking forward to another summer day of fun.

The bike ride was over three miles there and back. Mom didn't have to worry about the traffic because there were a lot fewer vehicles on the streets in those summer days. In fact, we rode in the street most of the time.

Upon arriving at the pool, I must have paid to get in but I have forgotten how much, probably around a quarter. If the cost to get in had been much more, I wouldn't have gotten to go. You could buy a season ticket for the whole summer but I never did.

Once you paid the attendant, usually a pretty high school girl, you were given a wooden hanger with a canvas bag attached for your street clothes. You changed in the dressing room and returned the hanger before heading for the pool.

There was a shallow concrete basin with special water to kill the germs on your dirty feet as you went out the back door of the dressing room. Most of the time, I was in such a hurry to jump in the pool that I would skirt around the basin on the raised edge so as not to get my feet wet. So much for clean feet.

A big deal was made back then as to how long you should wait to go into the pool after eating. The story was that you would develop stomach or muscle cramps and would drown if you went in too soon. This lecture was often repeated by adults, which scared us kids, but I can't remember anyone ever drowning because of cramps in the Delaware County pool. Another urban legend put to rest.

The lifeguards would blow their whistle every hour for the kids to get out of the pool for a rest period of fifteen minutes. But get this, then the adults got to swim in the pool all by themselves. The adults would lollygag in the pool going anywhere they wished. I think they were flaunting their *adulthoodness* in front of us envious kids.

We were always entertained at the pool by teenagers doing their heroics off the diving boards. Herby Johnson clowned around on the boards. He did a sailor dive from the high board, which was impressive and probably dangerous. For those of you who weren't there back then, a sailor dive is accomplished by diving head first into the water with your hands on your hips not over your head. Terry Johnson (no relation to Herby, at least I don't think so) was spectacular on jumping repeatedly on the end of the three-foot board until he got three feet above the board. The girls would watch him admiringly until the lifeguard blew the whistle and shouted for him to quit bouncing on the board.

I used to perform a mean back flip for the benefit of those clustered around the pool. Once you did the first one and knew how to do it, it was pretty easy. I never divulged that secret information to any of my buddies. I would stride out to the end of the board, turn with my back to the pool and balance my "athletic body" precariously on the balls of my feet with my arms extended shoulder high. I stood motionless in that position supposedly getting myself in perfect union with my inner self, until the planets were aligned in perfect orbit and the time was right astrologically, to begin. The truth was, I was seeking as much attention as possible before my feat. I pushed down on the board and let it spring me up and then I just put my feet over my head and voila, it happened.

You should not do a back flip from the high board (unless you are Herby Johnson). You may go over too far and hit the water on your back or belly which hurts like a son of a gun. The worst part would be that you don't look cool, which would diminish your pool persona with the fairer sex.

There were other places to swim in Delaware in that era. Blue Limestone was one. In the early 30's, Blue Limestone was a quarry. The State Highway Department was located there. In the forties and early fifties it was turned into a recreational area called Tilton's. There was swimming in the old quarry, horse back riding, miniature golf and a softball diamond located in the middle of it all. The local teams, mostly made up of veterans from World War II, played under the lights in the evening. Young Ohio Wesleyan couples could be spotted in the under growth around the park in the late evening. They were probably studying for exams.

One of the best places to swim was Eckel's Lake located south of town along the Olentangy River. It too, was once a quarry. It was rumored that an old Columbus, Delaware & Marion electric railroad car was at the bottom of the lake. How it got there was not part of the rumor.

As a kid, I would swim until my lips turned blue. It was a badge of courage back then. I stayed in the pool, no sunbathing or resting for me. Sissies used sun tan lotion, which was usually Copper Tone.

After a hard day's swim, I would ride home on my bike looking forward to supper and maybe after supper getting up a game of hide and seek in the neighborhood. Now that was a good ending to a perfect summer day.

HEROES

They say your values are set by age ten and your heroes at that age reveal much about who you are. I'm not sure who said that but it sure sounds profound.

At ten, my heroes were Roy Rogers, Gene Autry, Hopalong Cassidy, The Lone Ranger, (I thought it was The Long Ranger for years) Sunset Carson and Wild Bill Hickok.

All of them rode horses with fancy saddles and strived diligently to make the west a better place to live. They never smoked, drank, or chased wild women, at least in the movies. They never lost a fistfight, treated their horses badly or got shot. This is quite a feat because they were always getting shot at in every movie.

A lot of their time was spent getting on a horse then racing over the prairie and getting off the horse. Much of their time was also spent hanging out with the horses around the hitching post in the old western towns.

As I look back, my favorite was Hopalong Cassidy. He rode a big white horse with a silver studded saddle. He dressed in black with a hand-tooled holster that held two white pearl handled pistols. He had two buddies that rode with him. One was California, a short old man with a beard and a cackle for a laugh. Johnnie was the young guy that always got tangled up with the local schoolmarm. Roy and Gene used to do some singing around the campfire at night but I don't remember how the guitars got clear out there on the prairie.

It was rumored at the time that Gene gave the "King of the Cowboys" title to Roy before he went into the military for WW II. When he got back, Roy wouldn't give the title back. Just a rumor, so don't bet the ranch on it.

Sunset Carson's specialty was jumping off a roof onto his horse. I didn't realize how dangerous that was until I got older. It was probably hard on his horse, too.

Wild Bill Hickok wore his guns around his waist with the pistol handles facing towards the front. When he had to draw, each arm reached across his body for his guns.

As awkward as it seems, it didn't seem to bother him. He was still faster than the bad guy.

Sometimes during the movie, when the bad guys came in, we would hiss. Then when our hero came on screen we would applaud. That would be hard to do in today's movies because it's hard to tell the difference between the good guys and the bad guys.

The heroes of that time never killed the bad guys. They just shot the guns out of their hands and took them to the sheriff.

Now, many years later, I can say that my heroes acted honorably; no drugs, no booze, (they drank sarsaparilla) no scandals and no contract hassle over money. Cattle rustling and range wars are now memories of the past. Horses are seen only at county fairs and guns are considered bad karma. But I can still picture "Hoppy" sitting tall in his silver studded, black saddle on his white horse bravely facing the villains of the old west.

Interesting information from the inside cover jacket of Louis L'Amour's book: *The Riders of High Rock, A Hopalong Cassidy Novel.* The Hopalong Cassidy novels were written by *Clarence E. Mulford.* When he retired, he chose a young writer by the name of Louis L'Amour who wrote four more of the Hopalong Cassidy novels.

UNCLE JOHN

When I was growing up, Uncle John and Aunt Mill lived on a farm about three miles from Delaware. He would invite me out and I would get to watch him milk and feed the cows, slop the hogs and work the horses.

His horses were huge with big feet. When they were in their stall in the barn, I wanted to sit on them but was afraid. I would slip from one side of the stall to the other across their backs. They seemed tame enough but I was not used to being around horses. At the end of the day, Uncle John would let them out behind the barn in the pasture. Those big animals would be so happy to be out and free that they would jump and kick and run around with pleasure.

When you are a kid, a barn is a wonderful place. I would climb up in the haymow and swing on the rope pulleys that were used to stack hay. It was fun to just jump in the hay. Uncle John would let me throw down some hay for the animals. Boy, that was big time. I felt like I was really helping.

One day I rode with him on the manure spreader. He was cleaning up the barnyard and tossing the manure onto the spreader. Then we would go out and spread it on the fields. I remember him smiling at me because of the smell, but I didn't mind it.

One day I was coming from the house and a sow and her little pigs were enclosed in the area between the yard and the barn. I just climbed over the fence and headed for the barn. Only the big sow had other ideas. She didn't want me there. As she headed for me, I hightailed it back over the fence. I guess I learned not to bother sows when they had little pigs.

I enjoyed being in the barn when Uncle John milked the cows. The cows all knew when it was time to be milked. They would hang around outside, then when the barn door opened, they would lumber into their own stall. Every once in a while one cow would get in the wrong stall and a real fuss would break out.

It was my privilege to be invited to the farm for thrashing day. To this day, I'm not sure just what the farmers do on thrashing day, but I got a free meal out of it. All the women cooked the food and then served us outside under the shade trees. Uncle John had two other nephews from his side of the family who were close to my age so the whole day was a lot of fun.

Uncle John would haul grain to the grainery near where I lived in town. Sometimes he would spot me as he went by on his tractor pulling the wagon of grain. He would ask me if I wanted to ride back out to the farm in the wagon or on the tractor. *Wow, for sure, does the Lone Ranger where a mask!?*

One day my friend, whose nickname was Buddy, and I were headed for the movie theater, probably to see a western, when along came Uncle John and gave us a ride for a couple of blocks. Just as we were getting off, he asked if we wanted to ride out to the farm. This invitation took me by surprise and without thinking I said no thanks. My mind was set on a cowboy and Indian movie. Buddy said as we walked to the movie that we should have gone and he was right.

It wasn't long until I got a bicycle and a paper route so my trips to the farm came to an end. So now, I do wish that I had said yes and taken one last ride to the farm for another load of grain and another pleasant farm memory.

MEMORIES OF DELAWARE
IN THE EARLY FORTIES

In the early forties, Delaware was a quiet, small town. The war was going on somewhere "over there," so life was on hold. Husbands, dads, brothers and uncles were gone. Stars were hung in windows to show that the family had someone in the service. If the star was gold, it meant a person from that home wasn't coming back. One memory I have of Delaware during the war was the lines of people in front of the News Shop to buy cigarettes. They were rationed and very difficult to find or buy. If the News Shop got in a shipment, the news spread fast through town and people rushed to buy a pack. Dad would roll his own cigarettes and I thought it was great when I got to help him with the little roller.

Since our families, buddies and schools were here, Delaware was the center of our whole world. The only thing that told us about the outside world was the newspaper. Most of us kids just read the comics section, but I remember seeing pictures of tanks on the front page. I once asked Dad what was on the front page when there wasn't a war.

To get around town as a kid, you had to have a bicycle. Delaware was smaller in those days and had much less traffic, so bikes could be ridden safely all over town. Most kids had bikes and used them as their major source of transportation. Bike parking racks were everywhere: schools, movies, swimming pool and the bowling alley. Signs were posted downtown, "NO RIDING ON THE SIDEWALK."

Since this was before television, everyone read the newspaper. Paperboys had huge wire baskets attached to the front of their bikes for home delivery. There was the *Ohio State Journal* (the morning paper,) the *Columbus Dispatch* (the afternoon paper,) and the *Night Green* (the evening paper.) the *Night Green* was sold on the streets downtown. No home delivery. On Wednesday, the *Columbus Star* hit the newsstands. The most important paper, the *Delaware Gazette*, came out six days a week. If there was any fast breaking news, a special paper was printed and rushed to the streets. It was called an "Extra."

This gave us kids an excuse to yell, "EXTRA, EXTRA, EXTRA, READ ALL ABOUT IT," just like they did in the movies.

We had neighborhoods back then, not subdivisions. Many families rented. If someone had a mortgage, it had a bad stigma to it, like "mortgage hill" or "mortgage row." It meant the people there owed the bank. Banks were not utilized like they are now. There were very few checking accounts; everybody paid their bills with cash. Not everyone had a car as the neighborhoods were within easy walking distance of downtown. Many people walked to the movies and shopped downtown at The Peoples' Store, Wilson's Store, Delaware Hardware, and The Boston Store. There were two Five & Dime stores to choose from. The grocery shopping was done at neighborhood groceries. There were many small groceries spotted throughout Delaware and were within easy walking distance of where you lived. Many families charged their groceries and the size of these bills could be a hot rumor item in the neighborhood.

The Strand and Star Theaters were our main hangouts on the weekends. Admission was sixteen cents at the Strand and twelve cents at the Star. Movies were shown continuously from when they opened until the theater closed. Unlike today, it didn't bother us to walk in after the movie had started; we just sat down and watched until we came to the place where we had started watching and then got up and left. Usually, a double feature was shown and they changed three times a week. On Saturday afternoons, two western movies, a newsreel, a cartoon, and a serial were presented for the kids. You could see Roy Rogers, Gene Autry, Sunset Carson, Hopalong Cassidy and a host of other western stars. We knew their names, their horse's name and who their sidekicks were. We were confident in knowing they would always win. All westerns had some of the same lines, "You must be the new schoolmarm," "Cut them off at the pass," and of course, "Lowdown dirty sidewinder." Most of the cowboys sang, so the movies were sprinkled with the cowhands getting together with their guitars around the old campfire. We all wanted play guns for Christmas so that we could strap them on our hips just like Roy and Gene.

Ohio Wesleyan students were a part of the community then. The fraternity houses were in the residential north area of Delaware. The students were always flowing through the downtown area. Sometimes the boys, in their ROTC uniforms, would get together after class and march through town to their frat house. The students were usually from the east and wore expensive clothes. The freshman had to wear a red beanie hat. Saturdays in the fall were busy for Delaware. If Wesleyan had a home football game and Ohio State had a home game, downtown was a gridlock of traffic. There was no bypass at that time, so all the traffic went through the center of town. On Friday and Sunday nights, the "down homers" added to the traffic. They were people from Kentucky or West Virginia who worked in Detroit during the week and headed home on the weekend.

In that era it was fashionable for visitors to eat at Bun's Restaurant. And sometimes the line to get into the restaurant reached down Winter Street to Sandusky Street where the Boston Store was located.

If you wanted to come to or get out of Delaware, one way to do it was by Greyhound Bus. In a day's time there were five or six buses in and out of Delaware. You could ride to Columbus to work or shop and come back by bus the same day. The bus station was on the northeast corner of Sandusky and William Streets. Then it relocated to the corner of Spring and Sandusky Streets.

On Saturday nights, all the farmers, their families and the city folks, gathered downtown. They parked on the street (head in parking) for the great past time of watching the people walk by on the sidewalk. All the people would get together and discuss the war or crops or the latest items that were rationed. A trip downtown was not complete without a stop at the News Shop for a smoke, chew or a newspaper. If you were a kid and went with your dad, you might get a penny piece of bubble gum or a nickel candy bar. The evening was usually topped off with an ice cream cone from The Delaware Creamery on Union Street, followed by a slow walk home. As we made our way home, the sound of a train rumbling through Delaware might fill our ears. But there was no curiosity as to where the train came from or where it might be headed because we were home in Delaware and all was right with the world.

THE LATE FORTIES

After World War II ended, there were many changes from 1945 until 1950. Our country had just won the big World War. We were a proud and happy nation. The boys came home with great stories, along with back pay and enthusiasm to make up for lost time. They worked by day and spent their nights in the many local bars. At this time, smoking was cool and drunks were funny. A favorite tune was always blaring from the nickel jute box, "*Give me land, lots of land, under starry skies above, don't fence me in*." The G.I. Bill was putting a lot of boys through college that could never have afforded it. Some boys didn't come back to Delaware. They married girls from places like San Diego, Seattle or Norfolk and settled there, while many, sad to say were buried in far off places with names we couldn't pronounce.

After the War, the old ways were old fashioned. The times were changing fast as we moved into the fifties:

> Outhouses to indoor bathrooms,
> Two story homes to one-floor ranches,
> The quiet girl next door to blonds with dark roots,
> Prayer meetings to parties,
> Walking, to car ownership,
> Iceboxes to refrigerators,
> Roosevelt to "Give 'em hell, Harry" Truman
> Farms to factories,
> Housewives to working women.

The veterans married the girls that were waiting for them and started having babies at an alarming rate. No one knew if there would be enough classrooms or teachers when the kids started to school. The new generation was christened *The Baby Boomers*. Their parents were hell bent on giving this new generation everything that they never had as a child.

Against the post war backdrop, a ten-year-old kid in 1945 became a fifteen-year-old adolescent in 1950. The days of washing cars in the Olentangy River at Dennison Dam, buying peanuts from Red at his stand on Sandusky Street, and making fun of Callahan's shopping bags were gone forever.

New heroes appeared to take the place of the cowboys. There was Joe Louis, Vic Janowicz, Ted Williams and Len Visci (our teacher and coach.) Cars began to catch our attention, especially fast cars that could drag race from the traffic lights on Sandusky Street. Some of the cars had custom mufflers that gave off their own unique sound. We could tell who was going by, just hearing the sound of the muffler.

We discovered there was a big world outside Delaware. California was where everything was happening. That's where the movies were made, where everyone became rich and it was the pot of gold at the end of the western trail.

Joe Louis had three fights with Billy Conn. All of them were on the radio. We were learning to hate "Commies" as much as we had hated the Germans and Japanese. The atom bomb and Korea were on everyone's mind as we ended the forties and raced into the fifties.

JUNIOR HIGH

The sixth, seventh and eight grades were very busy years for me. It all started when I came home from school in the sixth grade and there was a bicycle on the front porch. Aunt Max had sent it up from Columbus. She sold my clarinet and purchased the bike. I had dropped out of band. Mr. Ross had made fun of me in front of the other band members so I never went back. I didn't realize it at the time but this bike would change my life. It was a used bike but in good shape. It had tanks covering the cross bars and a rack on the back for saddlebags or to carry a friend. My new source of transportation opened up a whole new life for me. This new mode of transportation would propel me out of the old neighborhood and broaden my horizons. I would leave my nickname, "Sonny," behind. My new friends would call me Gabe or Gabro'l.

One day, after school in the sixth grade, I rode over to the Dispatch newspaper office to see if I could get a paper route. Don wanted to go so he rode along on the back carrier of my bike. We both got paper routes. Mine was route #15. It was Franklin Street from William to Griswold, which included Court Street where the jail stood, then west on Griswold to Vanderman, along with Darlington Road. Don's route took up on Griswold where mine left off. His route included Vet-Ville, a little town of small trailers on Euclid Street where the veterans and their wives lived while attending Ohio Wesleyan.

I had the route for two years and nine months. Don't ask me how I remember that, I guess I was proud that I carried papers for that long. Sunday mornings in the winter were the worst. I had to get up early. It was dark and cold. My bike wouldn't work on the snowy streets so I had to walk carrying the heavy Sunday papers. It took me two trips back to the office because the papers were too heavy to carry in one trip. Some of the other carriers' dads helped them on Sunday. Dad told me that carrying papers was my job, not his. Don and I began to run around together. He had a distant cousin named Dale that moved in next door to him on Lake Street. Dale got a paper route also, so we became a threesome. I sold *Night Greens*, the evening paper, on the streets and in all the bars downtown in the evening.

Boy Scouts was another activity of mine at that time. The troop was #93. Doctor Crites, a local dentist, was our Scout Master. The meetings were held in the old William Street Methodist Church's basement. The church had a ping-pong table and Don and I became infatuated with the game and played it as often as we could. Ping-pong stayed with us throughout high school and we played it often at the Rec Center at old North School.

Moving to Willis High School from the sixth grade was a little scary. Willis was much bigger with many more students. We were divided up alphabetically and put in homerooms, where we went the first thing in the morning. The principal, Mr. Hopkins, gave the announcements over the speaker system to each room. Then we went to our classes in other rooms. In the beginning, we didn't know where we were going so things got tense. We soon learned where to go and we became more familiar with our new classmates. We felt excited when we were assigned a locker like the big kids. I remember we were so small that the bigger kids could push us into the locker and close the door.

During junior high, I was also in church choir at the Evangelical and Reform Church on the southwest corner of Franklin Street and Central Avenue. Mrs. Ernestine Pebbles was the choir director. Our youth choir made Sunday night trips to other churches in the area.

One of my big accomplishments in junior high was to tie the cloth belt of Kathleen Hayes' dress to the back of her chair without her knowing it. When the bell rang, ending the class, all of us sprang for the classroom door. Kathleen got half way across the room before she realized that she was pulling her chair.

In the eighth grade, I started noticing girls and had a few scary dates. In the ninth grade the girl-thing intensified along with sports and the coming together of a new gang. These new activities began to take up a lot of my time. The interest in Boy Scouts, choir and the paper route was pushed to the background and soon ended.

HOME ROOM 303

First row: P. Ray, P. Penn, A. Keller, A. Mascherin, A. Kelly, M. Miller, K. Ramsey, J. Roach, J. Morgan, R. Sheets, G. Rodman.

Second row: E. Roach, H. Krause, R. Piatt, J. Milla, C. Lumbard, W. Powers, C. McMullen, I. Russell, J. Jordan.

Third row: Mr. Rayburn, J. Kidder, M. Long, M. McKenzie, M. Parker, M. Kern, W. Porter, F. Joyce, B. Meyers, P. Sartwell.

Fourth row: B. Mitchell, D. Pickens, F. Moffett, H. Marshman, E. Madison, G. Shaw, D. McKitrick, D. Murfield, P. Orahood, W. Nease.

HOME ROOM 304

First row: A. Ward, A. Thomas, J. Vance, S. Terry, J. Watts, M. Swearingen, B. Tucker, Y. Spring, S. Wolford, B. Wickham.

Second row: A. Thomas, J. Swope, P. Wolford, S. Vogt, P. Vipperman, M. Welch, J. Stults, C. Welch, J. Valero, V. Smith.

Third row: M. Tillman, B. Williams, M. Shipman, L. Terry, R. Wolfe, L. Ufferman, R. Wallace, Mrs. Zerbe.

Fourth row: L. Thomas, J. Strimmel, N. Williams, P. Shively, W. Stevens, K. Van Brimmer, G. Young, K. Wells, B. Weatherall.

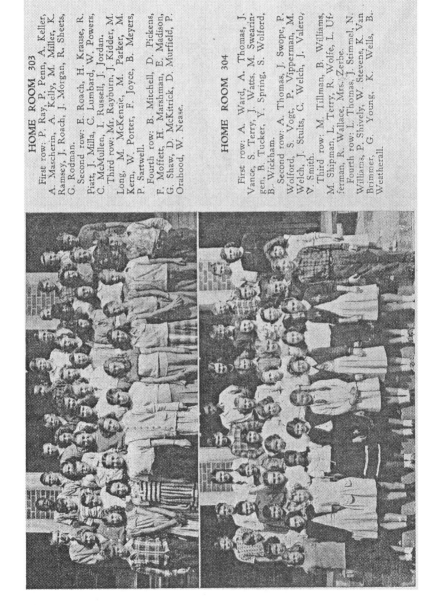

SEVENTH GRADE

HOME ROOM 301

First row: G. Crowl, T. Brown, J. Curtis, C. Culver, R. Blackburn, K. Breece, M. Banks, C. Courter, P. Call.

Second row: M. Cole, H. Brown, J. Farmer, P. Dunham, G. Breece, F. Boyd, D. Ballard, P. Davenport, H. Bame, T. Burroughs, C. Banks.

Third row: B. Bargdill, D. Easterday, M. Burden, R. Buford, W. Crump, D. Clark, F. Angelo, D. Arnold, P. Boring, R. Bennett.

Fourth row: J. Comston, A. Brown, L. DeWalt, N. Cross, L. Best, M. Dixon, B. Davenport, C. Butler, J. Campbell, R. Fisher, F. Blackledge, Mr. Felts

HOME ROOM 302

First row: M. Havens, S. Harter, K. Grandstaff, A. Hull, J. Glassburn, J. Hensley, S. Foreman.

Second row: G. Gale, L. Hamlin, N. Hilborn, K. Hayes, Y. Foster, C. Graham, K. Hamkins.

Third row: A. Hayes, C. Jones, C. Hipsher, O. Harrell, K. Gale, N. Hawkins, K. Green.

Fourth row: D. Jarrett, V. Hamlin, V. Hill, M. Fore, R. Gabriel, R. Jones, J. Jackson, R. Hagar, Mr. Johnson.

A SUMMER ON THE ROAD CREW

In the summer of my sixteenth year, I got my first real job. My dad got me on at the State Highway Department road crew for the summer. The crew cut weeds behind the guardrails and painted the guardrails and posts.

It was a fascinating summer of work, fun and with new experiences. The crew chief was a college professor and an ex-Navy officer. The crew chief never worked. We didn't care because he kept us entertained with his many stories of life in the Navy and comments on his life and times. He was a real man of the world, or so we thought.

Most of the crew rode in the bed of the truck, which had been converted with a bench seat on each side. There was one seat next to the crew chief in the cab. Two of us could and did sit on that one seat. I was usually the last one into the cab so I had to come in through the window and slide down onto the half a seat left with my right arm supporting me by holding onto the bottom of the open window.

We used scythes to cut the weeds. The implement, if stood on end, was as tall as we were. The first thing we would do after assembling the scythe was to sharpen the blade for about ten minutes with a sharpening stone. It was always a contest to see who could get their blade the sharpest and an argument always ensued with, "My blade's sharper than your blade." We would then get in a staggered line behind the guardrail. Each of us would have a row to cut. The old-timers on the crew that worked full time for the Department knew just how to gracefully swing the scythe to cut the weeds and leave them in a neat "windrow." This was a lost art that none of us high-schoolers ever mastered. We would beat the weeds into submission. We learned very quickly how to get a break from this backbreaking work; you just stopped and pretended to sharpen your scythe for another ten minutes. Sometimes you might shout something to a buddy so the old-timer could hear, "These dang scythes sure lose their edge quick."

Lunch hour was pleasantly passed under a large shade tree along the road while eating out of a metal lunch box. We played a cut-throat card game called hearts. Usually, the crew chief won, which added to our admiration of him and his conquest of the important matters in life.

We always had paint on us, so I am sure some of it must have been consumed during that memorable summer. At the end of the day, when we got back to the garage, the old-timers setting there would observe the splattered paint on our shoes, pants, shirts and hats, then dryly comment, "Get any paint on the guardrail today?"

At that time, the baseball All-Star game was played in the afternoon. Of course, we all became instant, avid fans and couldn't miss this important game. It didn't take much arm twisting to talk the crew chief into hiding out for the afternoon to watch, "The Game." The hard part was finding a secure, unobservable place to hide the state truck. One of the guys on the crew had a television, a rarity at that time, but the truck would not fit into his dad's garage. At the last minute, the crew chief volunteered to hide the truck in his secluded back yard. We thought we were really cool to pull this off.

The summer crew of the previous year had painted a pig, a legendary feat in our young eyes, until we learned that the pig died and they had to divvy up to pay for it. One day we were dispatched to bury a pig that had been killed on the road. We buried it, said a short eulogy and made a crude cross of sticks to mark the spot for eternity.

Part of the learning curve of new experiences was the fact that there were some real, live Catholic boys on the crew. It turned out that they were just like us; they wanted to laugh, joke around and have fun. Only, the crew chief slyly made fun of them all summer. We thought it was all in good fun but now, as I look back, it was cruel and mean.

The summer passed quickly as time does when you're enjoying yourself. September brought on a new challenging year of high school. There were new courses to take, girls to date and sports to play. The summer memories were swept quickly away. Only now, as I reflect back, can I fully enjoy again the laughter and good times of that special summer on the road crew.

THE GREEN SPLEEN

I remember my first car. It was a two door, 1937 Ford sedan. Under the hood rested an 85 horsepower V-8 engine. It was parked at the split of SR 42 and Horseshoe Road with a "for sale" sign in the front window. Dad and I drove out to take a look. Dad was a mechanic so he was my authority. I was also seeking his permission to buy a car, any car. After kicking the tires, looking under the hood and just walking around the car and staring at it, we bought it for forty dollars. I christened it, "The Green Spleen." This inspiration came to me because of the car's color.

Being only sixteen and new to driving, I had the task of learning to drive a stick shift car. The left foot would push the clutch and the right hand moved the gearshift while the right foot pushed on the accelerator. All this had to be done in perfect unison. If not, there would be a loud crunch of metal coming from the gearbox. It sounded like a meat grinder. Then a fellow passenger would chirp, "Grind me a pound." It was a fast car and I drove it with reckless abandon. If you drove over eighty miles an hour, it would begin to shake and the doors would quiver.

In those days, every time you pulled up to a traffic light, there was a chance for a drag race. We spent a lot of time in our cars. We were proud of them and they gave us a certain status. There was always three or four of us in the car. We would drive up and down Sandusky Street many, many times in the evening. This cruising would be punctuated by stops at the A & W Drive Inn to see who could chug a mug of root beer the fastest. These marathon driving sessions would also take us by various girls' homes. We would lean on our horns in hopes that this mating call would produce a female face at the window, or better yet, her emergence from the house to talk. To their credit, most of the "fem fatales" resisted the urge to materialize. Their moms probably advised them that proper girls didn't go out when boys honked.

Some of the guys worked on their cars. Sammy tore the motor out of his and did whatever you do to motors when you take them out. It took him all winter. In the spring, I went up and pushed his car with mine to get it running. We were all surprised—it ran. I never worked on cars. I did paint a 1939 chevy coup with a brush once.

The Green Spleen was temperamental so it began to have more down time than running time. The cost of keeping it going was more than I could afford, so I sold it. The last time I saw it was in Joey Chitwood's, *Daredevil Driving Show*, at the Delaware County Fair. It was used in the big crash scene.

I have had many cars since then but I will always have a fond place in my heart for the old Green Spleen and all the good times we had inside its quivering doors.

FOOTBALL FRIDAY NIGHT

The year is 1952, it's 11:30 pm on a Friday night. I am setting in the L & K Restaurant located in the heart of Delaware on the corners of Sandusky and William Streets. In the background, Johnny Ray is crying a tune from the jute box. I am devouring a toasted pecan roll and washing it down with a cherry coke. This snack will cost me 36 cents. A quarter for the pecan roll, a dime for the coke and a penny to the Governor. No tip of course. The jute box cost a nickel.

It's a football Friday night. The Willis High Panthers are undefeated. The whole town is excited. Some of the players are here smiling self-consciously as their fans shout, "Good game!"

There was a sock hop in the gym after the game. I dropped my date off; she had to be home by eleven. Now I am waiting for the guys to show up so we can see what's happening.

I bought a pack of Chesterfield cigarettes for a quarter from the machine in the back. I light one up with a large kitchen match by striking the head of the match with my thumbnail. I'm really looking cool. I have learned to blow smoke rings and to let the smoke drift out through my nose. Very classy. I willingly perform this feat in public to add to my coolness.

The L & K has floor to ceiling windows. I can set inside and watch the cars go by to see who's out cruising this time of night. Rosemary Clooney's voice is filtering through the restaurant with the song, *This Old House*, as the boys begin showing up after their dates or from cruising. About midnight we decide that whoever is not here, of our little group, is not coming. We discuss what would be fun to do. We could shoot down Route 23 to *Anntons* in Worthington for pizza, play cards somewhere, cruise around to see if we could pick up a drag race or we could get someone that looks eighteen to buy us a six pack of 3.2% beer. A whole car of us can get high on a six-pack.

Most of us have jobs that start early on Saturday morning but that doesn't cross our minds. It's too early to go home so we sit and sip our cokes and speculate on what to do.

When closing time catches us at one o'clock, we jump in someone's car that has some gas and cruise until two. If nothing exciting happens, we head towards home with the promise of meeting at the same place, same time tomorrow night.

RACING CARS IN THE FIFTIES

As I pull up to a traffic light on Sandusky Street, a look over at the car next to me reveals a contemporary glancing back. There are no words exchanged, like, "Do you want to drag race?" Your eyes have met and you instinctively know he is going to try and beat you away from the light. You both check the area for police cars or obstacles like a double-parked car in the way. Then you stare at the traffic light waiting for it to turn green. Sometimes as a taunt I race my engine a couple of times. If he responds in kind, it's a go for sure.

At the very first sight of the green light, you tromp down on the accelerator and drop the clutch. You both jump away from the light with tires screeching. As soon as your instincts tell you first gear is maxed out, you push the clutch in without letting up on the gas—then you slam the gearshift into second gear. This is called a speed-shift and if done right, the car will leap when you let out on the clutch. You don't glance over but you know you're leading by a couple of feet thanks to your superb speed-shift. His car is newer than yours, it's probably his dad's, so you know it won't take long for him to catch you.

Now you become aware that second gear is topped out, so you quickly speed-shift to third gear. There is no leap or jump this time but you're roaring along at a fast clip for a city street. About this time, you see the traffic light turn red at the next intersection. He has you by half a car length so you let up on the gas and down shift to second to let the engine slow you down. If done right, sometimes the muffler will make a cool popping sound as it backs down.

At the light you look over, smile and wave to your noble adversary. He smiles and waves back good naturedly. You make a right turn to split up in case you were spotted. You slowly drive around to let things calm down. The next time you cruise down Sandusky Street you may run into an easier match.

If you run into someone that wants to race and the police are cruising Sandusky Street you meet clear out at the edge of town on Troy Road between Central and Pennsylvania Avenues. It is a straight road, no traffic and only one house.

If you want to impress your buddies as to how fast your car will go, the perfect road is SR 42 south of town. From the city limits to the Scioto River is a seven-mile stretch of road, straight as an arrow with very little traffic. The thrill of the race is exciting and for a little while you get past the boredom that is a part of being a teenager.

WARNING:

**Don't try racing now, times have changed
and it's a different century!**

BOYS WILL BE BOYS

One summer evening in my high school years, five of us teenage boys were riding around in boring Delaware trying to find something to do. One of us suggested that we should go for a swim at the Delaware County Pool. It was around ten o'clock in the evening and the pool had closed at eight. Three of us climbed the chain link fence, took off all our clothes and plunged in.

I have one picture in my mind that has been there forever, it's of Sam standing at the end of the high board completely nude before he jumped into the pool. I have tried to erase that picture but it won't budge. It is always there for instant recall.

We had left two of our sneaky group outside as lookouts to alert us in case we would have to make a hasty retreat. Well, the sentries got into a highly competitive contest to see who could pass gas the loudest. As the three swimmers came back over the fence, we were informed that one of the contestants had over extended himself and a trip back to his house for clean shorts was necessary.

ARTHUR JACKSON FARMER

The other day I had the privilege of riding in a 1930 Model A convertible with a rumble seat. It had been nearly sixty years since I had ridden in a Model A. It seemed harder for me to get in and out of and the interior was smaller and more confining than I remembered.

Back in high school, Arthur Jackson Farmer had a 1931 Model A coupe. The car was in excellent condition. Jack, we all called him Jack, took excellent care of the vehicle and he would never drive it fast.

Once upon a time, Jack and I were in Columbus at the Ohio State Fair. We ran into a couple of classmates of ours, Connie Jones and Ann Sullivan. They needed a ride home so we all piled into the Model A and headed for Delaware, which was twenty-four miles away. Connie sat on my lap. By the time we got home, I was glad that Connie was thin and small boned because she got heavier the closer we got to Delaware. The fact that she was blond, pretty and the belle of our class helped my endurance.

Jack drove fifty miles an hour so the trip was not a speedy one. Sometimes Jack would put the car in neutral and let it coast down a hill. "This," he said, "saves gas." I am not sure he coasted on this trip. I will have to check with Connie or Ann, but they may not remember this obscure fact from the past. I am not sure why I remember these trivial old events. They are just there in the recesses of my unorganized mind. Could be age that brings these old memories up from the past.

Another time Jack and I were riding around after a snowstorm. We were cruising on Heffner Street. Jack put on the brakes while turning the steering wheel at the same time. The car spun around in the new fallen snow and was facing the other way. *Wow, that was fun*! We repeated that maneuver for the next ten minutes. The last time we spun the Model A, the tires hit the curb with such a jolt that it sprung the springs. One side of the car was now higher than the other. I still have the visual picture in my mind of Jack driving away after he let me out. The car looked like it was about to tip over. I think he had to hold onto the steering wheel to keep from sliding to the other side of the car.

Jack was stopped one night on Sandusky Street near the Police Station for excessive u-turns. A policeman saw him from the Station and came running out and wanted to know, "What the hell is going on?" For more details of this story, check with Phil Dunham. He was there. Phil, of course was quite familiar with being hauled off to the Police Station. He was involved in another suspicious situation the previous Halloween. Nothing ever came out of these two police incidents but the ugly head of suspicion still lingers to this day.

Jack and his Model A were included in a couple of episodes in our summer crew work for the State Highway Department. Work may be too strong a word here.

Jack, Bill Parker and I were going to ride home in the Model A after work. The car was parked near the Highway County Garage. Somehow, either purposely or accidentally, the vehicle got blocked in. Normally you would say, "Too bad, wait until someone comes." Nope, not us resourceful teenagers. We actually picked the front of the car up by the bumper and moved it out. Then we went to the back and moved it out the same way. We triumphantly drove away.

Another evening after work, we were driving down William Street by East School when flames and smoke came up around the emergency brake. We immediately opened the doors and climbed out on the running boards while the car was still moving. Jack must have had the throttle set because the car didn't slow down. He steered it from the running board with his arm in the window. We pulled in and stopped a block or so down the street to find out what was wrong.

The Model A was made so that if you so desired you could open the passenger door, get out on the running board, crawl up the front fender, walk across the front of the car on the bumper while holding onto the radiator cap, crawl back down the front fender on the drivers side, walk down the running board, step across to the rear bumper, then step back on the passenger side running board, open the door and get back inside. All this can be done while the car is in motion. All this sounds dumb, dangerous and silly but to young male teenagers it was a deed of honor and respect.

Herman Woulk lamented at the end of his wonderful Jewish romantic novel, *Marjorie Moringstar*, that time had passed the character by. Maybe he was the only one to remember Marjorie Morningstar: her beauty, the times, the fashions, the people and the events of that time in his life.

Who remembers Jack's Model A? Who was there then? Where are they now? Does anyone care or is it all buried with the past?

I remember and I enjoy running those precious innocent fun filled stories over in my mind; not unlike an old song that one enjoys hearing again.

As you can tell, I have many fond memories of Jack and his black Model A. My recent ride stirred up those good times and it was a pleasure to be reminded of them.

ONE SATURDAY NIGHT

One Saturday night while in high school, a painting party was semi-organized to paint the Hi-Y and Key Club meeting room. This meeting room for the two boys' clubs was located in the old high school at the back of Willis High School. The room was on the once condemned third floor. I believe it was rescued from condemnation for our use only. Nobody else wanted it.

About twenty of us gathered for the festivities in the late evening, around eleven. No adult supervision was present. We could not all paint at once. One of the guys had brought along some cigarettes, so some of us stood around smoking to look cool. Jerry, an upper classman, came over to our group to observe. Since he was older he was already cool, and therefore, trustworthy. He informed our motley crew that we were not really smoking unless we inhaled. He then showed us admiring lower classmen how it was done. After much watering of the eyes and coughing, we began to get the hang of it. Now we were cool, too, or at least we thought we were.

The Key Club color was light blue and the Hi-Y colors were maroon and gold. So that one club or the other didn't get offended, we painted the room in both clubs' colors. Can you even begin to visualize what a room would look like painted in those colors? After we finished, the full effect of the room could take your breath away. I never heard any comments from the teachers as to our choice of colors or painters, but I'll bet there was much head shaking and some sly grins exchanged.

At six the next morning, after the masterpiece was completed, I drove my buddies home. I pulled up in front of my house Sunday morning about 6:30 a.m. Mom was sweeping the front walk. My first thought was, "Wow, mom must have gotten up early." Well as it turned out, I had failed to inform them about the master painting party. They had been looking for me all night. In fact, they had even phoned the police with a description of the car and license plates. Needless to say, I was grounded. I was in the ground so far down, that you could say I was buried. All I needed was dirt thrown in on me. My teenage thoughtlessness had done me in again. I guess all great artists, painters included, must pay for their eccentricities.

THE REC CENTER

Long ago and far away in another time, there was a special place where a lot of teenagers in Delaware hung out. It was called, "The Rec Center." In the era of the fifties, we always had a place to go and there was always something to do and someone to do it with.

The Rec Center was in old North School on N. Washington Street. Before that, it had been located in the basement of West School and even before that, it was located on the second floor of the brick building on the southwest corner of Central Avenue and Sandusky Street.

The cost to get in was a nickel. We had to sign in for some reason, probably to make sure we paid. There was a bar for soft drinks and packaged snacks. There were rooms for dancing, ping-pong, pool table and a room for cards or chess. In the center, was a round main area leading to the various rooms like bike spokes to the outer tire. The center area had couches for reading or conversation.

The music from the dance room filtered out through the entire building. The popular dance step of the time was a step-hitch-step. The couples did this apart with arms around each others waist while both of you face forward, not unlike a team of horses. Then, after a couple of steps and hitches, the couple twirled and twirled until they went into a very accentuated low dip, with the boy learning the girl back until her eyes grew wide with fear of being dropped. After the spin and dip the step-hitch-step started again. I know this sounds awkward but it was really sort of fun and you could do the same step to any of the records of that time. Plus, we thought we looked pretty cool doing it. At that time, *cool* was the *awesome* of the teenage lingo of today.

The ping-pong room had three tables. You came in and if there was a game going on, you called, "winners," which meant you got to play the winner of that game. There could be three or four guys waiting to play, so they would play in the order they called, "winners." The more games you won, the longer you got to stay at the table but if you lost you had to call, "winners," and get in the rotation again. Johnnie Wing was flat out the best ping-pong player I ever saw at the Rec Center. Needless to say, he never had to wait in line because no one could beat him. Ken Creasy was good also and some others, but Johnnie Wing was, "The Man."

Sometimes we would play doubles with two on each side. Each partner took turns hitting the ball back. Getting around your partner to hit the ball back was the challenge and the noble opponent would hit the ball as far away from you as he could. Many expletives were mumbled as you tripped over your partner in pursuit of the elusive ping-pong ball. I would like to give you a detailed account of what went on in the poolroom, reading and card rooms but I have no recollection of the activities there. It seems like I was either chasing ping-pong balls or girls. Both proved elusive.

A saintly couple, Mr. & Mrs. Moore, volunteered their time so that we had a place to go and something to do. I would imagine that their volunteerism kept some of us from getting in trouble because we would have had too much time on our hands and nowhere to go. After I graduated, The Rec Center lasted a few more years but then it slipped away into the past where only our memories can bring it back as times changed and we moved on.

ONE MOMENT IN TIME

I received an e-mail the other day saying Andy Hull was to be honored for his athletic skills from his Willis High School days. That's great! Andy had quick reaction, was fast and very coordinated which made him good at basketball and baseball. He was All-State in baseball.

If someone were to ask me about who should be honored besides Andy, it would not take me long to go back in my mind's archives of special athletic contests and pull out one special moment in time. The sequence of events that threw two high school competitors together for something that can happen only once in a lifetime.

The game was tennis. The year was the spring of 1954. Two unnoticed, dedicated young athletes took the court to play second doubles together. This was their first start at varsity tennis. They both had put in their time on the bench watching and cheering those in the starting line up.

Now was their time! Can you imagine what must have been going through their minds as they took the press off their tennis rackets and stepped on the court? After all their sacrifice, they were finally there. Fortune had smiled on them.

These two young men proudly represented the rest of us at Willis High School. The fact that they lost the match, rather badly, should not affect our appreciation of their one moment in time when they gave their best for Willis High School.

GO PANTHERS!

The names of the two young men had to be removed due to a controversy of conflicting memories as to what really happened and whom it happened to. To me, remembering something that happened years ago is much easier then replicating a memory from last week. All of us have cherished, one of a kind, "moments in time" that might be more legend than truth. Be kind to us, it doesn't cost anymore.

This reminds me of a line from a John Wayne movie, *The Man Who Shot Liberty Valance*. "When the legend becomes fact, print the legend."

CHARGE, CHARGE
THE BLOCKHOUSE

When I was in high school, I majored in having fun. A friend of mine from the past told me once that I deserved to get an *A*. Needless to say, I didn't get into The National Honor Society. I wasn't even sure what it was.

One of my highlights was acting in the play, *Arsenic and Old Lace*. I lucked into the part of Teddy Roosevelt. It was an enjoyable part that got a lot of laughs and made me famous for the line, "*Charge, charge the blockhouse.*" I wasn't famous for the highest grade point, captain of the team or president of the class but, "*Charge, charge the blockhouse,*" was enough for me. When I first met my wife, who was five years behind me in school, she remembered me being in that play. Just think, if it had not been for *Arsenic and Old Lace*, I might not have won over my wife.

Many of the students were famous for various reasons. One of the young men from school was famous for riding his Harley motorcycle down the main street in town late at night while blowing his trumpet. Another fellow student was famous for his fast Studebaker and drag racing past the high school. Also, one big football player was famous for having heel plates on his shoes so that when he walked down the marble halls he made a cool distinct clicking sound. So you see, I was in good company.

Another exploit of mine happened at the 1954 Delaware County Fair. My friends and I wrangled a job seating people in the grandstand for four days of harness racing.

The management gave us these nice little white jackets with a green stripe. When we wore those jackets, we looked somewhat important, so the patrons could tell we were ushers.

Each day before the races, the announcer introduce the five queens that would rein over the races for that day. The queens were representatives of the local county high schools. They sat across the track in front of the announcer's booth in the infield. On Thursday, Brown Jug day, the queens were from Ohio Wesleyan University. I could see that the college girls were gorgeous, but it would be great to get a closer look. This is when I came up with a stupendous idea.

On the roof of the grandstand was a big enclosed press box. The management provided free Cokes for the press. Every once in a while the ushers would sneak up there and get a cold beverage. We had our little white jackets on so no one bothered us.

My idea was to go up to the press box, get five Cokes and carry them across the track to the beautiful queens. I couldn't carry five Cokes by myself so I enlisted the help of Wayne Lockwood. When we got up to the press box, one of the officials stopped us and asked what we were doing. I told him we were taking Cokes out to the queens. He said all right. He probably thought we had been ordered to do so.

We got the Cokes from the press box and elbowed our way down through the crowd. When we got to the gate next to the track, they opened it up as if we were royalty. We walked out on the track in front of about thirty thousand people and made our way over to where the queens were seated.

They were prettier than they looked from afar, all dressed up for their special day. They were also hot and thirsty so thanked us profusely for the cold beverage. It would have been embarrassing to just stand there and stare so we glanced at them, said thank you and returned across the track to where we were supposed to be.

I relate this story to you almost sixty years later because it is a cherished high school memory and one of my major exploits from that era. As I said, I majored in having a good time and this story is one of the reasons I deserved a grade of *A*.

DELAWARE WILLIS HIGH SCHOOL
CLASS OF 1954

Willis High School was opened in 1932 and was a high school until 1962. Then Rutherford B. Hayes High School was built. Willis was called *The Panthers* and the powers that be changed Hayes High School to *The Pacers*. This change was in keeping with the *Little Brown Jug*, which is the *Kentucky Derby* of pacer harness racing.

The era that was Willis was in the thirties, forties and fifties. The backdrop of national events during these years included, The Great

Depression, World War II, The Atom Bomb, The Korean War, The Cold War and Sputnik going up into space.

In the fall of 1947 the Willis High Class of 1954 left the protection of their local grade school. At that time the grade schools were named East, South, West and North. There was over a hundred in our class.

In 1949, Willis had a good basketball team and went to the district finals. Johnnie Johnson, the team captain, told us at a school pep rally, "Actions speak louder than words." The team played Columbus Central and lost. Our boys didn't shine that night, but Willis had a catchy, hard to learn, fight song that went:

> **"Our boys will shine tonight,**
> **Our boys will shine,**
> **Our boys will shine tonight,**
> **Our boys will shine,**
> **Our boys will shine tonight,**
> **Our boys will shine,**
> **When the sun goes down and the moon comes up,**
> **Our boys will shine."**

The styles of the time were girls in saddle shoes and full skirts while boys wore Levi's and white bucks as they scurried up and down the halls between classes, yelling at each other, carrying books, passing notes and holding hands with their steadies. There was always the constant clatter of slamming locker doors.

Delaware was a small town but we lived, worked, shopped and hung out in Delaware. In the early fifties we ventured to Columbus for that new thing called pizza.

The four high school years flew by with classes, sports, cars, dates, plays and part-time jobs. Then one spring evening, we rented caps and gowns and were marched down the isle at Gray Chapel and presented a diploma that declared we were ready to go out in the world on our own.

Each of us that attended Willis had a favorite teacher or coach that made an impression on us and changed our lives in some small way. As we look back, we come to the realization that the small connection made a huge difference later in our lives.

My teachers that made a difference were Miss Whitted and Mrs. Hearn. English Literature was the class Miss Whitted taught. I have no idea why I ever signed up for the class. The classmates that enrolled in that class were all brains and actually read books. After six weeks, I cornered Miss Whitted and confessed I wanted out. She laughed good-naturedly and said, "Ronald, you should stay in this class. It will be good for you." Well, I did stay and for the rest of my life, I have enjoyed reading books of all kinds. As for Mrs. Hearn, she cast me in various plays, which gave me the confidence to stand up in front of people without fear or self-consciousness. The confidence that she installed in me has helped me all my life.

Willis is still standing after eighty years. The building basically looks the same as the day we left. The wood framed glass doors, the marble floors, the light wood trim and the tall narrow gray lockers are still there. The older we become the more things change, so it's refreshing to find just one thing that has remained the same over the years.

The class of 1954 has remained remarkably close over the years. It is a pleasure to get together and exchange conversations on the past, where we are now, our families and their whereabouts. When we converse, it's as though time has stood still. We see each other as we were in high school. We take up where we left off like the time in-between has disappeared.

THE ROAD WEST

It was the summer of 1955. I had left home with a suitcase and a hundred and twenty dollars in my jeans with an adventurous dream to thumb west. The highway stretched before me like the yellow brick road drawing me to an unknown destiny and destination.

I had caught two rides from Delaware to Dayton, Ohio. The last ride let me out in downtown Dayton. I decided to buy a bus ticket to Richmond, Indiana. My plan was to walk to the edge of Richmond and thumb a ride on west. However, when I arrived in Richmond, I decided to go into the bus station and buy another ticket to Indianapolis. When the bus pulled into downtown Indianapolis, I was comfortably ensconced in my seat, so I bought another ticket to St. Louis. The bus arrived in St. Louis around two in the morning. No time to start thumbing, and besides, by now I had given up on the idea. Approaching the Greyhound ticket agent, I had to make a major decision. Do I want to go southwest to Joplin, Tulsa, Oklahoma City, Amarillo and Albuquerque, or do I go due west through Kansas City to Denver?

For some reason I chose Denver. The next morning I woke up in a super cooled air-conditioned bus cruising through the rolling hills of western Missouri.

The next night about 1:00 am the bus pulled into Denver, Colorado. After watching out the window at the bleak, baron, flat country of eastern Colorado, I had decided that I had seen enough of the world and when I got to Denver, I would turn around and go home. I was exhausted when I arrived so I thought I should get a good night of sleep before heading back home. I took a taxi to the local YMCA and got a room for the night.

The next morning after sleeping in a real bed, not a bus seat, I was refreshed and excited about being in a big western town that I had heard about all my life. I made up my mind that I should at least look around a little before heading home. The desk clerk let me store my suitcase behind the desk and I was off to see the city. I walked around admiring the new, tall, glass front buildings that were in downtown Denver. The city was a big, bustling, clean town. The buildings were newer than the ones in Columbus, Ohio. I eventually came upon a movie theater. *Mr. Roberts* was playing so I treated myself to a movie before the long trip back to Ohio.

After the movie, I was sauntering down the street gawking at the buildings and people, when I spotted an employment agency. Scrolled across the window in huge letters was "JOBS ON DUDE RANCHES AVAILABLE NOW." My reaction was, why not me? I went in and filled out a resume. I referenced my business school training and all the important jobs I ever had, such they were. A woman who was well over six feet tall called me in for an interview. She was dynamic with a booming voice. After she scrutinized my resume, she brayed, "Can you bus dishes?" I hadn't put down that I had worked at Bun's Restaurant during high school. I was too busy trying to dazzle the agency with my importance. I told her of my restaurant experience. She got up and came around the desk, towering over me she asked, "Are you fast?" "Of course," I answered. Then she asked if I could go to work tomorrow and leave this evening. I gleefully said, "Sure." She told me to be at the bus station at five for the ride up to Evergreen, Colorado. She said the resort that I would be working for, Troutdale in the Pines, would pay for the ticket.

At exactly five I was at the bus station looking for my ride. I walked past all the big buses trying to spot the one to Evergreen. The last vehicle in line was a six-passenger van marked Evergreen. The van pulled out through the busy Denver rush hour traffic. I had no idea what to expect. Soon we were climbing up in the mountains. I had never seen mountains before and the Rockies are impressive. I about broke my neck twisting around trying to see everything. The other passengers sat there quietly. They must have thought I was goofy, but I didn't care.

After about an hour, I was let out in a small primitive log-type western town. It was dark and a smattering of rain gave the town a desolate, lonely look. Someone was there to pick me up and take me farther up in the mountains to Troutdale in the Pines. When I arrived, they welcomed me with a smile, supper and a bus boy uniform. After supper, I was shown to my room in a log-type dormitory. My roommate was a happy fellow who was studying to be a priest.

I had left home on a Monday and I would be going to work in the beautiful scenic Rocky Mountains of Colorado on Thursday morning. *What an adventure!*

Don Byerly drove out two or three weeks later. He had wanted me to postpone my trip until he could go, but I figured if I waited it might never happen. Don got a job in Denver and came up on his days off.

A man named Margolous owned the resort. The guests mostly came from around Chicago, only, they sounded like they were from Brooklyn. I asked one of the girls why everyone talked funny. She just stared at me. Come to find out, I was working at a Jewish resort. I had read Leon Uris's *Exodus* so I wasn't a complete dummy. Uris had also written *Battle Cry* which was made into a movie. I liked the movie so I read the book. Battle Cry was the first book that I really liked, so it started me down the road to a lifetime of reading pleasure.

I was thrilled with the Rockies. We visited Red Rocks, an outdoor theater, and Central City. It rained a little every afternoon in the mountains. That summer was full of firsts for me. I saw my first Mexicans on the bus coming to Colorado. Also, there were two pretty Indian sisters from Oklahoma. I was fifteen hundred miles from home and having the time of my life.

Troutdale in the Pines was a summer resort, so they closed for the season on Labor Day. I was talking with one of the cooks after work one evening, lamenting as to what I was going to do after Labor Day. He said that the ski resort, Sun Valley, Idaho, stayed open until the fifteenth of October. I phoned the personnel man and he said to come on up because he had job openings. Don, a guy named Dick Anderson and I jumped in Don's car after Labor Day and drove nonstop up to Idaho.

We arrived in Ketchum, Idaho, which is located about a mile from Sun Valley. Ketchum was a small old western town. There didn't seem to be anyone around after dark so we wondered what we had gotten ourselves into. The next day we drove up to Sun Valley and were assigned jobs and a room. As in Colorado, resorts usually provide room and board with the job. When you work in a resort, you are a part of a big family of bellhops, bus boys, waitresses, maids, cooks etc. This makes for a friendly, open, social family of employees.

Sun Valley was owned and operated by the Union Pacific Railroad. Averill Harriman built the ski resort to emulate the ski resorts of Europe. The Valley was an "in" place for movie stars in the thirties and forties. Ernest Hemmingway and Gary Cooper hunted in the Sawtooth Mountain range surrounding Sun Valley. Among others, I saw Marilyn Monroe and carried James Arness' suitcases.

When we were there in the fifties, the area was still isolated, and sparsely populated. I had a small motorcycle that I used for exploring old, dirt, mountain roads and sheep trails. In the off-season the country was almost deserted.

The Valley was closed from October fifteenth until December fifteenth. Management gave us a free train pass home or to where ever we wanted to go. Don chose to go back to Ohio. I decided to travel to Los Angles to continue the adventure.

In the next two weeks I went to Salt Lake City, Las Vegas and Los Angeles on the train, then by bus to Phoenix, Albuquerque, Tulsa, Joplin and on back to Ohio. But that is another story.

THE CROSS COUNTRY GREYHOUND BUS RIDE

In the middle of October, 1955, Sun Valley closed for two months to wait for the snow for the winter season. Union Pacific Railroad owned and operated Sun Valley. The laid off employees were given free train passes home or to wherever they wanted to go.

I wasn't ready to go home. This whole western trip had been fantastic and I didn't want it to stop.

I took my free train pass to Los Angeles. The train went through Las Vegas so I got off there to look around. It was a Tuesday morning around 7:00 am. I walked up Fremont Street and the casinos and bars were open and busy just like a Saturday night.

The Horseshoe Casino had a sign out front saying that one million dollars was on display inside. I decided I wanted to see what a million dollars looked like, so I walked in. The display was right inside the door in the lobby. There was a tall, glass showcase with a million dollars in ten thousand dollar bills. I was standing there just staring at it when this guy came up and asked me how old I was. I told him, "twenty." He said, "Take a walk; you have to be twenty-one to be in here." As I walked out, I got to thinking, "What am I going to do in Las Vegas, if I can't go into any casinos?"

I decided to take a bus tour of Lake Mead and Boulder Dam. I got back in Vegas that evening and climbed on the train going to Los Angeles.

When I arrived in Los Angeles, I found I was in a seedy part of town. I located an old, cheap hotel for a few nights. I had originally planned to stay in Los Angeles and work for the two months until Sun Valley opened again, but by this time I was beginning to long for home. I decided I would look around a couple of days, then grab a bus for home. My free train pass ran out in Los Angeles, so the bus trip was on me.

For the next couple of days I took bus tours around the area. I saw movie stars' homes, the Hollywood Bowl, the planetarium where James Dean's movie, *Rebel Without a Cause,* was filmed. These places were all new and interesting but home was calling.

Late in the evening of my fourth night there, I journeyed over to the Greyhound Bus Station and purchased a ticket to Columbus, Ohio.

The first big city the bus stopped in was Phoenix. I got off the bus in the middle of the night because I had run out of money. I had a check from the Sun Valley Credit Union for $120.00 and it needed cashing.

I slept in the lobby of the bus station until the banks opened. I was awakened in the night by two policemen who were rousting this guy on the other side of the lobby. They didn't bother me, probably because I was Anglo and he was Mexican.

The next morning I walked around downtown Phoenix. The streets were wide and the buildings were new and clean. At nine, I walked into the bank. The teller sent me to the manager. He said he couldn't cash my check until he got written confirmation from the Credit Union in Idaho. He said he would advance me twenty dollars, and then send the rest to Ohio when confirmation came. He asked if I could make it home on twenty dollars. I said, "sure." I already had my bus ticket.

I went back to the bus station and grabbed the next cross country bus. One came through every twelve hours. The bus went north to Flagstaff and picked up the now famous *Route 66* which went east.

In some little town in eastern Arizona, the bus broke down. When we got off the bus, there were a group of Indians standing around. The Indians were short and had, what I thought, very unusual hats that were round, like a cereal bowl on the top with a wide brim circling it. The men's hair was long, in pigtails, sticking out below the brim of their hats. The women stood a step or two behind their men. They were talking in their own language, Navajo I think, and then they would smile or laugh every once in a while. I think they were enjoying this white man's dilemma. Our bus driver was talking on the phone. Then he would run out and work on the engine then go back to the phone to get more instructions. He finally got the bus running and we all climbed aboard, glad to be on our way.

About an hour outside Albuquerque, my tooth began to really cause me pain. By the time we arrived in Albuquerque, I had to get off the bus. The pain was shooting up and down my jaw. Of course, it was late in the evening. I didn't know what to do. I started walking around and finally I went to the Police station to see if I could get any help. By this time, I was pretty pathetic, what with crying and holding my jaw. They turned me over to a detective and he had no idea what to do with me. He took me to a Catholic hospital where a Nun gave me a shot that put me in la-la land. I thought the detective would take me back to the jail for the night. But he felt that that was not a good idea. So, the Nun said I could sleep in the lobby. At 6:30 am, a policeman came, woke me up and took me to the bus station. They wanted me out of town and I was glad to go.

The next night the bus pulled into Tulsa, late at night again. The shot of pain killer had worn off so now I was in misery again. I got off the bus and started walking around again not knowing what to do. I phoned home and asked if they could wire me some money to get my tooth pulled. Dad said he would, but it wouldn't get there until nine the next morning when the Western Union office opened up. So I walked and walked until I ran onto an old beat up hotel. They wanted $1.25 for the night. That was just right for my budget.

The next morning I picked up the money and headed for the dentist. He pulled my tooth. I gave him this long song and dance about not having much money, so he gave me a deal. After he pulled the tooth, he told me that I would have to go upstairs to another doctor and get a shot. Well, I told the other doctor that I had $15.00 to get me to Ohio. He charged me six dollars for the shot and I was on my way.

My big, super duper, double-decker, cross country bus stopped about every two hours for a break. Somewhere in Oklahoma, during one of my delirious nights, I was sleeping in a bus seat, which is not an easy task. When the bus stopped, I automatically got up to go into the diner. I was half asleep so I followed the woman ahead of me. All of a sudden, she slammed the door to the restaurant in my face. This woke me up, so I looked around to see what was going on. She was a black woman and had gone into the back door of the restaurant to the kitchen. It didn't take me long to realize that she couldn't eat in the restaurant with the other bus riders because of her color. This was very sobering to me. I had also seen a "whites' only" drinking fountain on this trip.

After Tulsa, the bus went on through Missouri to St Louis, then to Indianapolis and finally Columbus and home. My parents and sister met me at the bus station in Columbus. Mom said I looked thin. As Aunt Mill used to say, "Who ya tellin'?" We ate at Hall's Farm House on the way home. It felt great to be back in Delaware. The trip from Los Angeles had taken almost a week. What a trip! I will never forget it!

WINTER IN MIAMI BEACH

You would think after the long, hard, bus ride home from California I would want to stay home forever. Between Christmas and New Years of 1955, I read a classified ad in the newspaper that someone was headed for Florida and he was accepting riders for a fee. I phoned him and he said he was leaving for Gainesville in two days.

He picked me up early one morning. I had gone out and partied the night before. As soon as I got in the car, I fell asleep. The next thing I knew we were in Kentucky. I slept on and off the whole trip south. He asked me to drive in Georgia in the middle of the night. This trip was before interstate highway so we drove through every town or small burg. I was still pretty drowsy so the car wandered around the road a bit. Well, this seemed to bother him so he took the wheel back.

He let me off at the bus station in Gainesville, Florida, around 6:30 the next morning. I went inside and purchased a ticket to Miami. The previous summer, in Colorado, I had talked to a guy who had worked the winter season in Florida. That sounded cool to me.

The bus cut over to the coast and picked up US Route 1 and then drove through every town between Daytona and Miami. I arrived in downtown Miami at 7:30 in the evening on New Year's Eve. The city was crowded and booming. The Orange Bowl was going to be played there on New Year's Day. I had no idea where I was going to stay. I had not eaten all day because I put my money in my suitcase and then checked it through to Miami. If I picked up my suitcase, then I would have to carry it around until I found a place to stay.

I walked east a couple of blocks from the bus station and there was a huge Orange Bowl parade going down Biscayne Boulevard. There were lots of floats with pretty girls smiling down at the onlookers.

After about an hour of walking around, I finally found the YMCA and guess what, it was right across from the bus station! The man at the desk said they were full but then he must have taken pity on me. He said he had an empty bed, but I would have a roommate. At this point, anything sounded good.

I went back to the bus station, got my suitcase, and checked in the YMCA. Now, with the money from my suitcase, I went out and gobbled down a much-needed meal. At midnight, I was setting in a theater watching a movie. *Happy New Year*!

For the next few days, I walked all over Miami and even out to Miami Beach. In the local paper, I found a room to rent in a private house for $7.00 a week. The house was in Little River, a suburb in north Miami. A city bus line was close that ran out to Miami Beach.

I went to an employment agency and they found me a job busing dishes at a Miami Beach hotel. The name of the hotel was *The Tatum*. It was located three doors south of the Fontainebleau Hotel, which was one of the biggest and best hotels on the beach. The Tatum was a small, older hotel that I found out later was Christian. That means, no Jews were allowed to stay there. That bothered me some, but I needed the job.

The area I worked in, the dining room and lounge, looked out through huge, glass, floor to ceiling windows to the pool and the ocean. There were cabanas on each side of the pool. The dining room and lounge had fake decorative palm trees that made for a scenic atmosphere. Some days I would have the early shift so I would get to see the sun rise over the Atlantic Ocean. It was a memorable scene. That's what the guests paid for.

I worked January, February and half of March without a day off. One day I got tired and quit. For the next week, I went to the beach every day just like a tourist. I had contacted Don, at Sun Valley, the day I quit to see if he could get me a job out there. He did and said a free train pass would be waiting for me in Kansas City.

After a week of sun, sand and sea, I decided I had better hightail it for Idaho. I bought a plane ticket to St. Louis. The next morning I climbed on the plane ready to go. I began to worry that I was going to get sick. My stomach started churning around. Finally I said to myself, "You can't get sick setting here while the plane is on the ground. At least wait until the plane gets in the air." That reprimand calmed me down and I never thought about it again. When I landed in St. Louis, I put on my overcoat, gloves and hat, expecting it to be cold, but when I got off the plane it was sixty-some degrees.

I arrived in Sun Valley with a great tan, but was broke, because I had spent all my money on travel. The personnel director looked at me when I finally walked through the door and said, "Where have you been? We've been waiting on you for a week."

GARY COOPER

I was walking to lunch from the Lodge at Sun Valley, Idaho, to the Challenger Inn where the employees of the ski resort ate their meals. It had snowed the night before, then melted, and then frozen again. There were deep, frozen, tire ruts in the drive in front of the Lodge.

The walking was difficult so I was looking down to see where to step next so I wouldn't slip and fall. A woman's voice behind me loudly called, "Are you coming?" I looked around and the lady was looking directly at me. She was dressed like a skier so I decided I didn't know her. As I turned to trudge on, I almost ran into this guy. He was taller than I was so I had to look up. I immediately recognized him; had seen him many times. I knew him but he didn't know me.

He was Gary Cooper, the movie star, who I had seen in many movies. He was having as much trouble with the footing as I was. We looked at each other for a couple of seconds, and then I stepped by and went on to lunch.

THE LONG HARD ROAD

It was an unpleasant day in the summer of 1960 when my motorcycle sputtered to a stop. I was somewhere east of Boise in the rolling plains of southern Idaho. While riding east, I could see the rough outline of the Sawtooth Mountains far off to the north.

The August heat reflected off the road up at me like a slap in the face. The day before I had ridden the 180 miles from Sun Valley to Boise. The capitol city of Idaho had not been my destination but for some reason I went for a ride and just kept riding. Have you ever wanted to do that? I located a cheap room in a rundown roadside motel at the edge of town. In the evening I toured the downtown and took in a movie.

The next morning I lit out for Sun Valley. I was supposed to have been at work by eight that morning. I wasn't going to make it. Around ten miles outside the town of Gooding the bike came to an unscheduled stop. It was the kind of bike you had to kick-start just like Marlon Brando had to do in the movie, *The Wild One*. I kicked and kicked but it wouldn't start. Finally, I pushed it down a lane to an old ranch house. The farmer that lived there said I could park it there until I returned.

I walked out to the main road and started thumbing the hundred miles back to Sun Valley. The first ride took me ten miles to Gooding. I walked through Gooding to the east side of town and proceeded to thumb my way to Shoshone were I would turn north up Route 93 to my destination.

The sun was high in the sky as the white clouds with dark blue bellies drifted lazily by. I was sweating and the heat from the road came up through my shoes like I was standing on a hot stove. Two hours dragged by as many motorists passed by without stopping. The people would glance over at me then quickly look away. I found out later, that a couple of weeks before, a hitchhiker had killed a good Samaritan who had offered him a ride.

Finally an old man in an old pickup truck stopped. He had farm produce in the bed of his truck that he was taking to a farm market on up the road. He drove maddeningly slow and would even have to shift into second gear to get up some slight hills. But I thought, *at least I'm moving*. After about an hour, I had begrudgingly adjusted to the speed of 25 miles an hour, then we had a flat tire. I thought, *am I never going to get back to Sun Valley?*

The old man got out two small axle jacks. Each had about an inch diameter top to hold the weight of the truck. The jacks had to be placed just right under the leaf spring. To accomplish this, you had to lie flat on the ground and place the jacks in just the right place under the spring. The jack must then be raised by hand as far as it can go. The next jack must then be inserted under the next leaf spring and pumped to it's maximum height. I thought the old man knew what he was doing so I just watched. By this time I was really frustrated by the whole time consuming situation. Then the truck slipped off the jack and just about came down on the old man.

I said, "Let me try." I was disturbed by the whole mess and I was going to show the old man how quick I could change the tire, being young and all. I adroitly slipped down under the truck, placed the first jack in just the right place, then pumped it up to it's full height. I then placed the second jack under the next leaf spring and raised it quickly to it's full extension. I jumped up and swaggered around the truck to remove the flat tire, but the truck wasn't high enough off the ground. The jacks were as high as they could go. I had no idea what to do. In fact, I said to the old man, "What are we going to do now?" The old man casually remarked, "Dig out from under the tire." I just stared at him. Maybe the old man wasn't as inept as I thought after all. At top speed, I dug out from under the tire, pulled the flat tire off, put the new tire on, unjacked the jacks, put the tools away and jumped in the truck ready to roll at whatever speed the old man wanted.

When we arrived in Shoshone, the old man said he was going to get the flat tire fixed and if I waited he would run me on up the road. I pictured getting back to the Valley in the middle of the night so I thanked him kindly and said, 'No thanks."

Outside of Shoshone, I caught a ride in a new Buick and the driver clipped along at eighty all the way back to Sun Valley. I walked into the employee's cafeteria, hungry, sun burned, tired and humbled by the old guy who taught me a life's lesson I never forgot. Youth doesn't know everything and never under estimate your seniors. I had taken one small step down the long hard road to adulthood.

THE GOOD SAMARITAN

One September night in the late fifties, two friends and I were driving back from Twin Falls, Idaho, to Sun Valley. As we drove up the road into the mountains, the car began to sputter and jerk. We finally pulled off the road. Don went around and pulled up the car hood. I leaned on the side of the car, smoked a cigarette, and moaned about being stuck in this desolate place without a vehicle that worked.

A car pulled up and a man leaned out the window and said, "Are you having trouble with your car?"

Don said, "Yeah, I think it heated up coming up the mountain."

The man said, "Can we help? We could take you to the next town."

Don replied, "No thanks, I think if we let it cool down, then start it back up, it will be fine."

The man said, "Ok, if you are sure."

"Yeah, thanks for stopping."

The man who stopped was Ernest Hemingway and his wife. Afterwards, I thought we should have taken the ride even if our car did work. Then we could have said that we rode with Ernest Hemingway and people would listen to our story and be impressed. We could have been somebody, but no, Don had to say, "No thanks." Don and I have known each other for over sixty years and I have never forgiven him for passing up a chance to ride with Ernest Hemingway.

FOOT NOTE

In that era, in the rugged rural Sawtooth Mountains where Sun Valley is located, there wasn't any fawning adulation of famous people. I remember standing next to Hemingway in line at the local drug store. He waited in line like everyone else. No one came up and asked for his autograph or gushed over him. He and I had a brief conversation but I can't remember what it was about. Probably it was about the great American novel or something like that. I also saw him in the local western bars with his friends. He always carried a sheepskin wine sack which he would squeeze until a stream of wine would shoot into his mouth. I am pretty sure he was given a break on that. If I had carried wine into the bar they would have, not so politely, asked me to leave!

HOMEWARD BOUND

I was speeding down a mountain road in Idaho, late at night in the winter of 1961. The accelerator was reacting to my heavy foot. I was enjoying the thrill of speed and the 1953 Oldsmobile was instantly responding. The snow was piled along the road like mounds of white sugar. The moonlight reflecting off the snow gave an eerie glow to the countryside. The view out the window was going by like a video on fast forward. I was relaxed and happy from my evening of partying. That was, until the right front tire slipped off the road. My driver's training class had taught me to not pull the steering wheel back quickly but to wait and ease it back onto the road. But before I could do this, I hit a built up driveway and was catapulted into the air and across to the other side of the road. The car flipped over three times and took out 120 feet of fence and two telephone poles. The car ended up on its' top with me in the back seat. When I crawled out unhurt, I noticed the steering wheel was almost against the front seat. If I had not been thrown in the back seat, I would have been killed. The car was totaled. For the next few days the people that saw the wrecked car would look at me like I was a ghost. The car was not insured and I had to pay for the fence and telephone poles. If I had not known the local sheriff, I would have spent some time in the hoosegow.

The accident gave me cause to examine my life and its' direction. In the spring, I stepped aboard a train in Shoshone, Idaho, called the Portland Rose, and headed for Chicago and home. I knew that I would not be returning to these scenic mountains. This phase of my life was over. The accident brought it to a close and could have brought my life to a close as well. Now I am homeward bound to begin a new life.

Little did I realize at that time that I was leaving a part of me in Idaho. In years to come, when the dentist was drilling my tooth, my mind would revert to Sun Valley for peace and refuge. When the politics of my work would close in and almost suffocate me, I had a place to retreat to. I would picture myself on my small Zundap motor cycle exploring the old mountain roads and trails of central Idaho. The years that I spent in those picturesque mountains and the people I met along with the memorable times I had were a constant crutch of support for me for the rest of my life.

Hemmingway wrote profoundly about the area when his friend was killed in a hunting accident in the 1930's:

"Best of all he loved the fall,
The leaves yellow on the cotton woods,
Leaves floating on the trout streams,
And above the hills, the high blue windless sky,
Now he will be a part of them forever."

THE STATE HIGHWAY DEPARTMENT

In the spring of 1962, I decided to try to get a job at the Ohio State Highway Department. Dad had worked there for 39 years, until his death in 1961. Jobs out there were very political so I had to go see the Delaware County Democratic Committeeman. His name was Bob Parker and he was the owner of Parker's Men's Clothing store. He put in a good word for me.

The Personnel Director at the Highway Department wanted to put me on the sign crew, but I had decided I wanted on a survey crew. I held out for the survey crew and got hired after pestering them for three months and passing a civil service exam.

Working on the land survey crew was interesting. The work was outside in the fresh air and not confining. We surveyed for highway projects like new, small bridges in rural areas and right-of-way markers. I tried to learn as much as I could. I practiced writing my numbers so they looked neat in the survey notes we took. Surveying was mentally challenging and diverse, so the day's activities were always fresh and new.

The crew chief worried about me around the road traffic because of my eyes. He took me in the office for an interview with the engineer of the Right-of-Way Department. I did not want to be transferred inside to an office job. I went to the crew chief at his home and pleaded with him not to transfer me. He did anyway. Little did I know then that the transfer was a great career opportunity for me in the coming years with the Department.

My first assignment in the Right-of-Way Department was to go to the six county court houses in District Six and trace land titles back to verify who owned the land and if they had a clear title. I knew nothing about this procedure but I was fortunate enough to work along side a nice old man who was patient and knowledgeable. While in this department, I started taking educational courses that the Highway Department offered.

After doing title work in Right-of-Way for three years, I moved over to Relocation, which was helping people who were displaced by highway projects.

I really liked real estate appraisal work because it was like detective work figuring out land values. My courthouse background helped me by knowing how to look up recent land sales and what they sold for. I took many land appraisal courses and was finally switched to the Appraisal Department as a real estate appraiser.

From there, I continued to work myself up the ladder. If there was an opening, I went for it. The process usually consisted of going to someone higher up in the organization and telling them my qualifications for the job and how good I would be at it.

My really lucky break came when the Real Estate Supervisor position came open in District Six. I had left the District 17 years earlier in my upward movement quest. I had worked all over the state in various positions. The Ohio Highway Department was now called The Ohio Department of Transportation and the Right-of-Way Department was now called Real Estate. After being interviewed by The Director of The Ohio Department of Transportation, on the seventh floor in Central Office in downtown Columbus, I was told I had the job. My new office was the same office that I was interviewed in when I was transferred from survey crew twenty-eight years earlier. My last years would be back in Delaware from whence I started. I had made a big circle.

I retired from ODOT in November 1994, after thirty-three years. I went out on my own and did real estate consultant work for eleven more years. My last project was a bike path in Delaware, Ohio. On that project I did the title work, appraisals, negotiations and the closings; the complete real estate procedures for the project, all on my own.

COFFEE

The first thing I do each morning is to brew myself a pot of coffee, usually five cups. It was six, so I am improving. I drink all five cups before I start my usual unproductive day. This morning process caffinates me up to the edge of the shakes.

I use a special brand of coffee called Community Coffee. It is processed in Baton Rouge, Louisiana. I stumbled onto it's robust flavor when we were in New Orleans. Robust is a word that is always used when talking about coffee.

Would you believe that at one point in my life, I actually paid a nickel for a cup of coffee? Now the menu in a restaurant reflects $1.75. I asked the waitress if that was a misprint? She gave me a hostile stare and very condescendingly said, "No sir, that's the price." I ordered water.

In high school, my school days' breakfast consisted of two Chesterfield cigarettes, a cup of coffee and a day old cream horn from Bun's Bakery. My mother worked in the bakery and got to bring home the day old baked goods as one of the benefits of the job.

I think the reason the young people rail at us oldsters and think of us as cheap is because they weren't around when a candy bar was a nickel, a gallon of gas was a quarter and a movie cost sixteen cents. Today's general run of the mill young people don't have those figures to compare present prices to. Poor things. If we seniors are ill mannered enough to mention the high cost of things, we are given that disgusted, be patient with the old folks look.

Did you know a bottle of water at an Ohio State football game costs $4.00? I am talking about *water*. Ounce for ounce you could drink beer cheaper.

My mother drank cups and cups of coffee. There was always a pot of coffee on the stove. The old drip kind. So whenever someone dropped in, and in my mother's home it was often, the visitor was offered a hot cup of coffee and an open heart.

When I first got married, I would make a full pot of coffee on the weekends in case anyone dropped in. They didn't. I found the drop-ins came to see my cherished mother.

In frequenting the trendy coffee establishments, I find that the best are the ones who roast their own coffee beans right there on the premises. The fresher the roasted bean, the better the *robust* flavor of the coffee. My theory is that Starbucks roast their beans in Seattle, then send them east by wagon train. It's hard to tell how old the roasted bean is by the time you drink it.

These are serious matters for us coffee nuts but for the non-coffeeaholic public they probably seem trivial. Mark Twain was reputed to have said, "If they don't make a good cigar in heaven, I choose not to go." My rendition of that quote is, "If they don't make a good cup of coffee in heaven, I choose not to go."

MILK

When I was a kid, milk came in a glass quart bottle. A milkman delivered the milk to your door. In the early forties, in my neighborhood, the milkman was Skip Glassburn. He made his deliveries with a one-horse milk wagon. He lived on the southeast corner of Central Avenue and Union Street. Don't look for his house now because it's gone. They tore it down in 1961 to make room for the new improved Central Avenue bridge and four-lane street. The new Delaware Municipal Building is now on that very spot.

Good old Skip set the milk on the front porch. In the summer, we would quickly put it in the icebox. No one seemed to worry about the milk spoiling on the front porch before we picked it up. In the winter, the milk would freeze in the bottle. The cream would separate to the top of the bottle and when it froze it would push the cap up a couple of inches above the bottle. We thought this looked cool. It didn't bother us that the chemical structure of the milk might have been compromised.

They tell me the milk in that era was not pasteurized. As a kid, I thought this meant that the cows weren't allowed in the pasture field. My Uncle John had cows and we got to drink the milk right there in the barn. Cows were neat, they smelled good, and they didn't bite. Even the grain Uncle John fed them smelled good. I always wanted to eat some but never gave it a try.

When I was in grade school, they served us milk in little cardboard containers. It was usually lukewarm and I hated it.

We used to drink whole milk, the next change was to drink 2% low fat milk; then 1% low fat milk. After that came total fat free milk. Now we drink organic fat free milk. By now the poor milk is so diluted it tastes like flavored water.

I really don't care because I only put milk on cereal. The cereal covers up whatever taste the milk has left. Every once in a while, I have an organic fat free glass of milk with a sweet sugary donut.

The last and final step is to do away with milk as we know it and manufacture it with chemicals. I think we are almost there.

SHOE BOXES

I have this thing for shoeboxes. You might call it an obsession. Shoeboxes appeal to me because they are just the right size to store my treasurers in. They are not too big so as to be bulky and not too small or odd size to be worthless.

A nice size shoebox is a thing of joy. You can even store shoes in them and they stack up symmetrically and are visually pleasing. Shoeboxes are the perfect size for mailing gifts. I tell you now, right out, shoeboxes are one of technologies greatest accomplishments in the modern era.

I get a shoebox every time I buy a pair of tennis shoes, or as they are now called, sneakers. The term "tennis shoes" dates me. I wonder if "sneakers" derived from the fact that if you are wearing a pair of them, you can *sneak up* on some unsuspecting soul. It's something to think about if you can't fall to sleep some night. And now that I think about it, I haven't bought a pair of leather dress shoes in over ten years.

When the shoeboxes start piling up in the closet and then on the workbench, I still find it very hard to throw a box away. I know I will get another box when I buy another pair of shoes, but my insecurities take control.

The next time you purchase a new pair of shoes and blithely, unemotionally, discard the container, think of me.

WASHING MY HANDS

The older I get the more I wash my hands. Society and my wife have pressured me into this ritual. The fear of germs increases with age. I shudder remembering how many times I didn't wash my hands as a kid. I am slowly becoming Howard Hughes. The next step will be to let my hair and fingernails grow long. Come to think of it, my hair has a good start.

I wash my hands before each meal. If I'm at a restaurant, I come back to the table with my just washed hands held high like a surgeon walking into the operating room. I think it's funny but after sixty seven times my wife isn't impressed anymore.

When men go to the "John" they are supposed to wash their hands. "Supposed to," are the key words. I seem to be subliminally alert for the guys who don't. I believe this reveals a character flaw in the transgressor and from that day on, he is on my, "don't shake hands with list."

Just for the record, men don't strike up conversations with other men in the restrooms. Not a comment about the latest ballgame or the weather—nothing.

When I take my five-year old grandson into the restroom, he pumps a full white glob of soap the size of a small egg into his hand and proceeds to wash. He loves the blow driers, which I despise. There should be a law that all public restrooms have paper towels for drying hands.

After I wash my hands in a public restroom, then comes the problem of the door handle as I leave. I have observed that certain despicable varmints don't wash their paws and then they grab the door handle—disgusting! I still have the paper towel that I have just dried my hands with and I use it on the doorknob so I don't have to touch it. But then everyone in the restaurant can see the paper towel in my hand when I come out the door and I am exposed as a germ freak. Plus, what do you do with the towel. Life is not easy for a Howard Hughes wannabe.

There is another major decision men have, what do you do when you go into the restroom with dirty hands? Do you wash your hands, then do your business, then wash your hands again?

In my short time on this planet, I have observed that farmers and doctors are the most thorough people in washing their hands. They even wash the backs of their hands up to the wrists. Mechanics also do a decent job, but they have the advantage of seeing what they missed.

Science has come up with the hand sanitizing lotions. When applied, they are supposed to cleanse the hands of 97.5% of all germs. The lotion can be purchased in small bottles so you can carry them with you. My criticism of the lotion is that after you apply it and you don't wipe your hands, those dastardly germs are still there somewhere. If they are dead, then their little bodies are still there.

I wonder if my diligence in the pursuit of germs will help me live a longer, or a happier life? Time will tell. Right now, Howard Hughes seems more of a burden than a hero.

MUSIC, MUSIC, MUSIC

I drive a 1992 red Chrysler La Baron convertible. The top is down most of the time. In fact, it sits in the garage with the top down, ready to go. I named the vehicle, *The Red Baron*. One of my many quirks in life is naming my vehicles. My first car was named, *The Green Spleen*. I once had a red chevy caprice aptly named, *Zelda*, and a big Dodge diesel truck that was called, *Brutus*. The truck was a brute that pulled my thirty-foot fifth-wheel camper, which was named, *The Orient Express*. The truck's name also had a close association in my heart with Ohio State's *Brutus the Buckeye*.

The other day I was driving The Red Baron down to the library. My destination reveals my age, but who cares. The trip was an excuse to drive around with the top down and listen to my fifties music. I was driving around listening to those quiet, melodious tunes of old when the thought struck me; *I was driving around listening to this music fifty some years ago in high school. So what has changed? The circle is complete.* The next step for me is to drift back to grade school. Maybe I can learn my multiplication tables this time. I did pretty well until we progressed to the twelve's. I never learned the twelve times whatever. I have to say five times twelve is sixty, then figure out what I want from there. Anyway, I'm not going back. I will just apply for an educational grant from the government to learn multiplication tables. There's grant money for everything else, why not multiplication tables.

I'm getting off the subject of driving down to the library with the top down and fifties music blaring. *What coolness, what pizzazz!* Younger motorists give me questionable stares; I feel sorry for them. At least I can understand the words and the music is not hard on my ears.

The love songs of the early fifties insinuated that if she gave in life would be wonderful forever. The two of you would drift off into a dream world unmoored to earth or reality:

> **"If you do what I am dreaming of,**
> **life would be a dream sweetheart.**
> **Sha-Boom Sha-Boom**
> **I'll do anything for you,**
> **anything you want me to.**
> **All I want is having you and**
> **Music, Music, Music"**

If I were pushed to choose a favorite singer of the early fifties, it would have to be Nat King Cole. His soothing voice was always accompanying events of our lives and he defined the seasons of the year.

It's not Christmas until I hear Nat King Cole sing:

> **"Chestnuts roasting on an open fire,**
> **Jack Frost nipping at your nose,**
> **Yuletide carols being sung by a choir**
> **And folks dressed up like Eskimos"**

Summer hasn't arrived until I hear:

> **"I love those lazy, hazy, crazy days of summer.**
> **Those days of picnics, pretzels and beer."**

Fall is here when I hear:

"The days dwindle down to a precious few,
September, November
And these few precious days I'll spend with you,
For soon we'll hear old winter's call.
But I love you most of all, my darling,
When autumn leaves start to fall."

Who didn't believe Nat King Cole when we were sixteen and he crooned:

"They try to tell us we're to young,
Too young to really be in love,
They say that love's a word,
A word we've only heard,
But can't begin to know the meaning of."

We knew it all at that age and what we had was the real deal no matter what our parents said.

Before you think that I have lost it completely on the early fifties music, I didn't like Spike Jones or Bing Crosby. I know it's un-American not to like Bing but he was too "croony" for me. And what's with the name "Bing?" Where did that come from? I did like Johnnie Ray but he cried a lot for a man, but hey, we can't all be John Wayne.

But alas, in 1955, Bill Hailey and the Comets thundered onto the music scene with *Rock Around The Clock*. This record changed everything and started the rock and roll craze, which doomed my kind of music. My music only lasted a short time; from the end of the big bands in the late forties until rock and roll got going in the mid fifties.

Now I ride around in The Red Baron resurrecting the great melodies of the early fifties that I grew up listening to and hoping that someday someone will yell out their car window and say, "Hey, I remember that! Sounds great! They sure don't make music like that any more!"

AUNT MONNIE

Aunt Monnie came floating down the river in the 1913 flood. At least that's what my grandparents told the other siblings. Their favorite story when another new baby was born was that they dug him or her up out in the horse stall. Mom said she and her sisters spent many hours digging in the stall looking for a baby.

Aunt Monnie was one of nine children so she learned to stick up for herself early, whether at the dinner table or in the yard playing. This attribute never left her for the rest of her life. She was feisty, quick witted and an extremely independent person. Her whole family was loud, boisterous and enjoyed a good laugh. If there were four or five of them in the same room, they would all be talking, each getting louder and louder in order to be heard. Of course, each one felt what they had to say was the most important.

Aunt Monnie was about five foot three inches tall with short brown hair and was a little plump. She had a very challenging attitude. She would ask me if I had read the morning newspaper and if I said that I had, she would ask if I had read this or that article. Of course I had hurriedly browsed the paper and had to say, "no." Then she would say, "I thought you said you read the paper."

She worked as a bookkeeper, a telephone operator, and other jobs. She also handled all of her and her husband's finances and business affairs. They never had children. Her husband died when he was only fifty-two. They lived on a five-acre track of land in the country.

When her husband, Uncle Bill, was drafted in World War II, he wanted her to be with him. By the end of the War, she had been in Alabama, Washington D.C. and New York City. She never talked about her travels. I don't think she saw anything that impressed her. She felt that

Delaware County, Ohio, had everything to offer that anyone could ever want. My mother had that same attitude.

One time my sister and I were drying dishes while Aunt Monnie washed. I said, "Aunt Monnie, there is something still on this plate." She answered, "It's a poor dryer that can't get his half." My sister and I loved it and always quoted that comment from that day forth.

One of Aunt Monnie's jobs was a telephone operator for Ohio Wesleyan University. She worked in the basement of the venerable old Gray Chapel. The building was one of the original buildings on campus. By the way, as the old family story goes, the Chapel was "supposed" to have been built with quarried stone from my Grandfather's quarry. Late one night she closed down the phone switchboard to leave. When she got out in the hall, she smelled smoke. She went back in and called the fire department. They came, found the fire and put it out. They said if she had not called, the whole building would have gone up in flames. Aunt Monnie was written up in the *Delaware Gazette* as the woman who saved Gray Chapel.

When Aunt Monnie was forty-five, she was diagnosed with cancer. She was taken to a special hospital in Columbus for radiation, which was very new at that time. I was young so I can't remember what type of cancer she had. In the fifties, we were afraid to say the word cancer. We just said C or nothing at all, usually nothing at all. When Aunt Monnie was in the hospital, Uncle Bill came in one evening and said he had paid all the bills by check. Aunt Monnie asked him if he had checked the balance in the account; later they had to go to the bank and borrow enough money to cover all Uncle Bill's checks. Aunt Monnie beat the big C. The following year she went to the doctor for a check up. He told her she was cancer free and she was written up in the books as a case study. She lived another twenty-nine years.

One day Aunt Monnie and I were talking about a certain person. She warned me, "Watch out for him Ronnie, he's slippery." I have used that term many times since then.

I borrowed Aunt Monnie's car to bring my wife and new daughter home from the hospital. We had a little Volkswagen with a poor heater and it was January.

Aunt Monnie decorated the graves before Memorial Day. I helped her do it when she got older. It was a hoot. We took flowers, watering cans, a little shovel, gloves, plastic bag for the weeds, folding chairs for breaks, coffee, drinking water and donuts.

I have decorated graves with my wife, who is very precise and systematic. The flowers must be arranged by color and the same number must be planted on each grave so no one would feel slighted. The weeding must be accomplished so that you get the full root and not break it off. I lose valuable points when I break off the roots.

Anyway, Aunt Monnie and I lugged all this paraphernalia to the cemetery, then Aunt Monnie just sort of threw the flowers in the ground. I guess she figured she got them this far and it was up to the good Lord to do his half.

My fondest memory of Aunt Monnie was being at the graveyard with her. We would talk about family and who was buried where. She would tell me old stories about growing up on the farm. Thinking back on those days at the cemetery always brings a smile to my face and sadness to my heart that she is gone and I am reminded of how much I enjoyed her and how much I miss her.

OHIO IN THE FALL

BEST OF ALL I LOVE THE FALL

Long walks down narrow, quiet, tree lined country roads. Green leaves turning yellow, gold and crimson as they picturesquely cling to the trees until the first cold, windy, rains of November charge down from Canada.

Bright yellow school buses picking up happy, excited, chatty, eager children waiting beside the road while tearful parents wave goodbye.

A disappointed dog walking back down the lane alone after a summer of companionship.

Teenagers grooming and showing their animals at county fairs.

Costumed little beggars with their brown grocery bags, scurrying down streets lined with bright porch lights inviting them in for Halloween treats.

A huge full moon illuminating the whole landscape like a giant flood light.

Brilliant, round, yellow and maroon mums smiling out from frostbitten flower beds.

The excitement of Ohio State football! The thrill of the team and band in their colorful uniforms coming out of the tunnel onto the green, grassy field at the *Horse Shoe* as 105,000 standing fans roar their approval.

Pumpkin pie with a dab of whipped cream and a cold glass of apple cider.

In the fields, the tall corn turning yellow from the bottom up and the soy beans turning yellow from the edges in as they patiently wait to be harvested.

Bright sunny days followed by clear, cool nights that are perfect for sound sleeping.

Oh, yes, best of all I love the fall.

EAST SCHOOL

I remember attending old East School,
where the three R's were taught as a rule.

Our teachers there stayed a very long time;
all of them made us tow the line.
There was MacElvain, Sipes, Warren, and Crisswell
who taught for a generation and did so well.

But the master of all, the principal in fact,
was Mr. Conger, no doubt about that.
He was dynamic, tough and tall,
and we gave him no lip at all.

In the spring, his favorite poem he'd read
about a barefoot boy, a creek and a creed.
The very next day, we would follow his lead
and come to school barefooted,
for he had planted the seed.

As I look back now, on those wondrous years,
he seemed larger than life, the man of our fears.
It was him who shaped our experiences there,
in study, in sports, and the stories he'd share.

In tribute, above East School, is written his name.
A hard, rugged man, who deserved the fame.

AS TIME GOES BY

One Saturday morning in the spring, I decided to ride my bicycle down to the Hamburger Inn for breakfast. The restaurant is under new ownership and is supposed to be new and improved.

My morning ride took me by Jane M. Case Hospital, where I was born a few years back. The facility is now called Grady Memorial. The word on the street is that Jane M. Case donated $500.00 years ago so the Hospital was named after her. But along came Mrs. Grady and her estate left the Hospital two million dollars. Everybody forgot about poor Jane and immediately renamed the hospital.

On my way down Central Avenue, I turned on Euclid Avenue, which is also named Pacer Way after the new high school which was built in 1962. I rode one block on Euclid Avenue, oh excuse me, I mean Pacer Way and turned on Griswold. This maneuver gets me out of the traffic on Central Avenue and I also get to enjoy the beautiful old homes located on Griswold and Franklin Streets. Most of these homes are in perfect condition for their age and are pleasing to view for their architectural design. My paper route was along these same streets back in the middle 1940s. I believe these homes are in better condition now than they were then.

When I reached the downtown area, I parked my bike in front of what used to be Zack Davis's seed store and Joe Vogel's Peoples' Store. I locked my bike to the bike rack located on the sidewalk. While growing up in Delaware, I never had to lock up my bike. In fact, none of the other kids I knew locked their bikes.

I walked over to the Hamburger Inn. A new maroon awning shaded the front window and sidewalk where some tables and chairs were available for diners to eat outside. It was reminiscent of a French Café. La-de-da!

Upon entering the restaurant, I spotted the newly painted red walls along with recovered stools and hanging lights. The menu was the same. I ordered two eggs, hash browns, (they give you about a half a pound) and wheat toast. When my order arrived, I cut up the eggs and hash browns and mixed them all together. As the yoke of the eggs mixed with the hash browns I shoveled a fork full of this ambrosia into my mouth followed by a bite of toast and a swig of coffee. *Ecstasy—life is good.*

The counters are U shaped so you are looking directly into the faces of the diners across from you. I find this somewhat disconcerting but it doesn't seem to bother the other customers.

The Hamburger Inn has been a traditional landmark in Delaware since the early 1940s.

I can remember going to the Star Theater for twelve cents and then dashing down two doors to get a candy bar at the Hamburger Inn. It was a hole in the wall then with one counter running front to back. There was a neon sign in the front window that said, "Hamburger

$.05," but later the sign was covered with a piece of cardboard. I guess hamburgers had gone up and they hadn't replaced the sign.

For the last seventy years, the restaurant has been the place to go for breakfast or just coffee and conversation. The men, and now women, gather at the back counter to thrash over their opinions on politics, weather, sports and rumors on the latest happenings in Delaware County. It doesn't matter what your status is in life, when you enter the Hamburger Inn everybody is equal in who you are and what you have to say.

The Hamburger Inn is famous for a spicy hot bowl of chili. In my high school days, we would enjoy seeing an unsuspecting Ohio Wesleyan University student wander in and order a bowl of chili for lunch. We would remain quiet while the student downed a couple of spoons full of the steamy brew. Their expression would turn to alarm as they quickly reached for a glass of water. Then we would hee-haw. It didn't take much for us to enjoy ourselves in those days.

For years, the Sunday morning ritual in our house was to go downtown and buy a paper from the News Shop and then go across the street and purchase a few fried cinnamon rolls from the Hamburger Inn.

Today, the downtown is decorated with white merchant tents for an arts and crafts street fair taking place this weekend. I walk briskly up and down Sandusky Street viewing all the priceless wares displayed, only to find that there is nothing I can't live without.

As I walk down Winter Street past the Strand Theater, which is about to become new and improved, *Robin Hood* is now playing. This must be the forth Robin Hood movie in my life span. Can't they get the story right? There is a rumor that Robin Hood never existed. After four movies about him, I personally don't care.

On the way back up Winter Street from a book sale at the Library, I was trying to traverse the obstacle coarse of people and food trailers, when I hear the sound of a live swing band coming from the parking lot behind the Bank. I make my way over and there is a five-piece band;

drums, trumpet, saxophone and two guitars. A talented black woman is singing some blues. They are really good. I stand transfixed and listen. It is the best band I have heard in Delaware since Ray Anthony's band played, *When the Saints Go Marching In*, at old Edwards Gym in the early fifties. The group is smiling and moving to the music, enjoying themselves and their music. It is good to hear some live music for a change.

While making my way back to my locked bicycle, I notice that to be really cool at an arts and crafts street show you must have a dog with you, preferably a big dog and it helps if the dog looks hot and thirsty. Also, it is a must to have a couple of small children with you. To be super cool, the kids should be pulled in a little red wagon. Well, I don't have a dog or kids so I decide to, "get out of Dodge."

Upon arriving back home, I was pondering my adventure to the new and improved Hamburger Inn and my observations on the day's ride. The thought hit me that I have become too critical. I have aged into a geezer. Usually the term is used with *old*. As in *old geezer*. I think old in that context is redundant. I am not sure how the female population got a reprieve for not being labeled, geezer. Anyway, forgive me for my sarcasm and for thinking the past was best. As time goes by, I find myself clinging to the past for support as the world rushes on.

CHRISTMAS 2008

Joyce and I spent Christmas in Beaufort, South Carolina. Our wonderful daughter lives there with her two offspring, our only grandchildren. Ian is five and Grace is four years old. This is the perfect age for Christmas and believing in Santa. When they get older, in the first grade, the other little rascals will squeal about Santa and his chimney routine and reindeer on the roof baloney.

Our daughter married a man with five children. The oldest is, John, who is 23 and in the Marines. He has had a tour of Iraq and is now stationed in Okinawa. The next oldest are 21 year old twins. Paul is at the Navel Academy and his sister, Mercy, is studying animal husbandry at Clemson University. David is 19 and also attends the Academy. Ruth, the youngest, is 13 and still at home. The first five children have biblical names. Our first grandchild is a boy and is named Ian. Steve, our son-in-law, wanted to name his youngest daughter, our 2nd grandchild, Grace, so that Mercy and Grace will follow him all the days of his life. We are, of course, very proud of our grandchildren, but also very proud of our step-grandchildren. Since we had nothing to do with their upbringing, we feel we are not bragging on their wonderful accomplishments as they have all worked very hard to be where they are in life. All of the family will be home for the holidays including, our son-in-law's parents, Fran and Mary Lou Eklund, who are from Wisconsin and wintering in Ocala.

THE BIKE

We came home from eating out; an often occurrence when in St Petersburg. Not cooking at home is so frequent that I hide things in the oven that I don't want Joyce to find. While we were gone, one of the neighbors in the park had put a small two-wheel bicycle on our patio under the carport. The bike was colorful and looked brand new. After tracing down the benefactor, we learned the bike had been their granddaughter's and she had outgrown it. The bike did not have training wheels and it was just the right size for Ian to learn to ride.

The bike was loaded into the van for the trip to Beaufort along with Christmas gifts, luggage, food, extra toys to keep the grandchildren entertained, and anything else that would enhance the holiday season in South Carolina. The van was packed full. Joyce and I had just enough room to squeeze in the front seat. Every time we go to or from Beaufort or Ohio, I think, *This time we won't have much to take*, but the van always ends up full.

Can you remember when you first learned to ride a bicycle? The feeling of excitement and freedom was all consuming. I learned to ride on my cousin Geneva Louise Evan's bike. I pushed it up and down the sidewalk on Liberty Street. I would run along beside the bike and then jump on. When the bike slowed down and was about ready to fall over, or worse yet, crash, I would jump off. I proceeded to balance myself a little longer each time and to pedal just once. Finally the balancing and pedaling was shakily mastered and I was riding. It was a right of passage.

I worked with Ian for about two days. I would walk behind him and keep a hand on his shoulder to give him the feeling of balancing and slowly pedaling. If you remember learning to ride, the hard part was starting and stopping. He did crash a couple of times. He would jump up, look himself over and say, "no blood," and try again. After his completing two days of training, Papa retired to the couch. The real reason I quit was because he was getting better and I had to pick up my speed from a walk to a trot. I believe in sacrificing for my grandson, but I draw the line at a heart attack.

The day we left for our return trip to Florida, Gigi said that I had to see Ian on his bike. I pictured myself beside him at a fast jog. I grudgingly went out front to the road. To my surprise, my handsome, athletic grandson was riding his bike up and down the road. The starts and stops were unconventional and his turns a little shaky but he had wheels and he was on the move. The most poignant vision of this event was a blissful expression on his little face. "Look out world, here I come!"

CHRISTMAS AT BURGER KING

Our first assignment, upon arriving in Beaufort, was to occupy Ian and Grace so their mother could prepare for all the holiday festivities. It was greatly appreciated that we got our grandchildren completely out of the house. The longer they were away the better. The first day for lunch we went to Burger King because they have an inside play area and the grandchildren love it. Have you ever spent two and a half hours at Burger King? I think not. My food and coffee consumption was punctuated by happy shouts "Look at me Papa!" Papa is the endearing nickname that my grandchildren have christened me. Sometimes they call me Pops. I am happy to answer to either summons because I know that I am about to receive their full attention.

I would like to state that the time spent at Burger King with the grandchildren was quality time that I will always remember and hope that they have a special place in their hearts for Papa and Gigi. Gigi is Joyce's special nickname which signifies Grandmother Gabriel. In a perfect world the above would be true, however, I would like to note that the coffee was really bad and the play area was noisy and to tell you the truth, I got a little bored. So having said this, the very next day when the assignments were passed out at the family homestead, guess who got the kids! And guess where we went! Back to the tried and true BURGER KING, only this time we only stayed an hour and a half.

We then ventured to the Water Front Park on the bay in downtown Beaufort. The Park has a terrific children's play area, which is adjacent to a sumptuous coffee shop where the lattés are worth the trip to Beaufort. We spent close to two hours at the Park and I didn't mind it at all. There were other grandparents there fulfilling the same assignment as we were so all of us felt useful. I just want to know one thing, where were all these super play areas when I was a kid? Our parents sent us to the movies or outside to play in the yard or the empty lot down the street.

CHRISTMAS EVE

My daughter entertained a small intimate group of fifteen for a Christmas Eve meal and opening of gifts. There were the seven children, the other set of grandparents, son-in-law, Steve, and JeMelle, a semi-resident teenage girl who is staying with Lisa until she goes off to school. JeMelle is no trouble because she is always talking on her cell phone; I think even while she is sleeping. Rachel, a 21 year old friend of Lisa's was there also. They both work at the local health food store. Their love of health food binds their friendship.

The activities took place in four areas. The television was in one half of the great room with Steve, his dad and the boys circling it like an old wagon train in a Western movie. The other half of the great room was where the Christmas tree and presents were. The food was on the table in the dining room. You could come and fill your plate, then find a place to sit and eat. Lisa, her mother, mother-in-law and Rachel were mostly in the kitchen and the rest of us would wander in with our humble request for more food or drink.

After the meal was served and the presents opened, the kids played with their new toys throughout the house. About the same time, the Karaoke serenading commenced. This means we had the television with the Karaoke, the women in the kitchen exchanging recipes and the very excited grandchildren bouncing around in anticipation of Santa. Papa took his plate of food and hid out in the dining room.

The evening ended when the young adults circled through the house giving hugs, smiles and goodbyes. Not unlike birds in the fall, circling, gaining numbers and momentum, then heading south. After they left, and the young ones were tucked in their beds waiting for Santa, the house became quiet and seemed empty, so we all went to bed hoping that Santa wouldn't hurt himself coming down the small chimney.

HUNTER

During the hectic activities of Christmas Eve, there were recurring mummers about Mercy's boyfriend, Hunter, being due to arrive in Beaufort to meet the family on December 27th. There was anxious anticipation as what to expect. The name, Hunter, to me conjures up visions of a country club tennis player or even worse, a golfer. I was hoping he did not have three names like Hunter Randolph White. You just can't trust a guy who has three names.

Well, the evening finally arrived and Hunter made his appearance. He was not what I expected. He was my height, slight built and seemed relaxed and easy going among the large boisterous family to which he was introduced.

He had a rural North Carolinian accent with a slow, soft-spoken drawl that captured your attention. You could listen to him talk all evening. Hunter wore his ball cap all evening in the house. He also drove a pickup truck. What more could you ask of the kid?

As the evening progressed, we found out that Hunter had a great interest in old blues and instrumental music of the forties and fifties. In fact, he played one of his homemade CDs for us.

Hunter mentioned the name Earl Bostic, who, he said, was the best saxophonist he had ever heard. I asked him if he had anything new out, and Hunter said that Earl died a long time ago. I googled Earl Bostic and Hunter was right, he must have died years ago because there were no live videos of him on the Internet. You could listen to some of his records, but that was it.

The evening ended with Mercy's three brothers challenging Hunter to a pool game at the local sports bar. I had the feeling that as quiet and unassuming as Hunter is, the brothers had better keep their money in their billfold.

After the group left, Lisa and her mother cleaned the kitchen, tidied the house and imprisoned the grandchildren in their rooms so Papa could enjoy some much-needed peace and quiet.

THE ENDING

On the drive back to St. Petersburg, Joyce and I reflected on all the activities that took place in one short week while we were in Beaufort for the holidays. It seemed the time just flew by; we just got there, and then it was time to come back. We were busy every waking minute and some sleeping minutes too. A couple of mornings when I woke up there were four in the bed. I was clinging to a small area at the side. Relaxing while Joyce drove, I felt like a soldier that had just been pulled from the front lines and sent to the rear for some R & R, (rest and recuperation) and I sure needed it but what a wonderful Holiday it was.

THE CHOCOLATE
PEANUT CLUSTER CAPER

At a recent bake sale auction, we purchased a plate of chocolate peanut clusters. We really didn't want sweets around but the auction was for a good cause.

The plate was beautifully wrapped with clear cellophane and a bright red ribbon with a bow. It looked colorful and appetizing setting on our coffee table.

My wife and I were keenly aware that these clusters were not a healthy choice item. The plate was on the coffee table to entice our holiday guests.

We knew the dastardly effects that these innocent chocolate delights have on a weight watcher's plan. We also had an unstated commitment of chastity.

A remarkable, even mystic thing began to happen. Over the following days, clusters began to disappear one at a time. To add to the shocking mystery, the cellophane and the red ribbon with a bow seemed undisturbed. The plate appeared undisturbed.

My lovely wife and I did not broach the subject as to the demise of the peanut clusters.

As the days passed, so did the number of missing chocolates and the plate cover remained intact. The plate now has only one cluster remaining. My plan is to rip the cellophane and ribbon off the plate, consume the last lonely cluster and never bring up the subject of the chocolate peanut clusters again.

CASE CLOSED

THE REST OF THE STORY

However, a neighbor came over to watch a football game and when he left, I noticed that the last cluster was gone!

JOHN ADAMS

I stumbled onto a copy of the book, *John Adams*, last summer at Krogers for $15.00. The book is written by David McCullough. It was first published in 2001. I don't usually get around to reading a good book until there is a lot of publicity and many people have recommended it. This process takes from five to ten years. Oh, yes, they have to make a movie out of it and then I say to myself, *"Read the book first, then you will enjoy the movie more."*

I started reading this 651 page book reluctantly. However, I found that I really enjoyed it. It was interesting to read about the men and of our country's inception. To know that if it weren't for these great men sacrificing their time and energy this nation would never have been founded.

I have been reading this book for four months. I have interrupted it a couple of times to read two of my fluffy detective novels. Now I seem to only read it when I do the laundry. I figure I am reading the book an hour a week. I am on page 224 and I have around 400 pages to go. If I read ten pages a week, that would take around forty weeks to complete. I will forget the beginning of the book by the time I reach the end. I know you may say read some in bed each night, but I fall asleep.

One of the advantages to this long read is that I leave it out in a prominent place on the coffee table so our acquaintances, who come and go, see it and know that I am reading a historical masterpiece. Then they think, to themselves, that I am doing something to improve my mind. They chide themselves that they should be doing something like that too. Also, when I talk to people, I casually bring up that I am reading, *John Adams*. This has the effect of getting a glimmer of respect, or is it resentment? The only thing about this scenario is that it could turn ugly. For instance, I was talking on the phone to my cousin's husband, Ed Hanlon, when I dropped the remark that I was reading *John Adams*. He said, "Oh, yes, you mentioned that to me on the phone when we talked last month." I had been found out. It was embarrassing.

Whatever the motivation of mine for embarking on *John Adams*, my motives are pure and my eyes are clear and keenly sighted on my ultimate goal. So if I casually mention to you in a couple of years that I am reading *John Adams*, just nod your head knowingly and say, "That's great."

SENIOR EMPLOYMENT

I was talking to Don the other day and he was lamenting that if the stock market gets any worse we may have to go back to work. This statement got me to thinking. What would Don, Phil and I do if our many skills were called back onto the open employment market?

I have scrutinized our qualifications and scoured our separate resumes in search of some, or any, redeeming work skills for which an employer would compensate us. It finally dawned on me that we all worked for the Ohio Highway Department in the summer while in high school. We painted guardrails and cut the weeds around them. I think the Mexicans have the landscaping business pretty well covered now. They are hard workers and seem like nice people, but we still could do the painting. Except now the heavy traffic on state routes and the speed they drive while talking on cell phones would make it very dangerous for us seniors with less than fast reaction time. We would be like sitting ducks.

So I went back to my research, and lo and behold, I found that Phil was once employed by the City of Delaware as the chief and only maintenance man at Mingo Park. With Phil's exemplary qualifications, Don, Phil and I could approach The City of Delaware to be the new maintenance crew for Mingo Park. If the City bulked at our request, we would use the ever effective *"Senior Card,"* which is: three financially strapped seniors trying to remain independent and support themselves. If that doesn't work, we would threaten to contact the Federal Fair Employment Agency to investigate the City to see how many seniors were gainfully employed by them and to see if their hiring practices were prejudicial to seniors. The "age" block should not be on the job application. If we allow that, before long they would want to know if we were physically able to perform the work which is a direct violation of our personal rights. After we politely explain all this to the City, I am sure City Management would see the light and give us a contract to maintain Mingo Park.

Once we have secured our contract, we will immediately apply to the Federal Small Business Administration for a loan with the premise that we are putting seniors back to work and creating jobs that will produce income tax revenues for the Government.

Since Mingo Park is adjacent to the Olentangy River, which is a designated "scenic river" through Delaware and that Mingo Park is the only park in Delaware that is on the river, we would apply to the Ohio Department of Natural Resources for a, "*PRESERVE*," designation. After we receive the, "*PRESERVE,*" designation, we will request to The National Park Service for a grant to enlarge our small Park because we feel that there are endangered animal species or flora fauna, indigenous to this area that should be protected at all costs.

At this time, we come to the realization that total security is needed to protect the park from poachers and marauders. This means a huge grant from Homeland Security for a perimeter fence and a gatehouse to regulate the general public from entering and disturbing the area.

The "*PRESERVE*" will now need a new administration building. We will approach the senior Senator from Ohio to include our extravagant new structure in the next pork barrel bill going through the Senate. Oh yes, we will name the building after the humble Senator from Ohio, which will be a sure way to expedite the funding.

Our final act will be to apply to the Bill Gates Foundation for state of the art surveillance cameras, computers and a phone system. During the negotiations, it would be mentioned that a lot of Gates' grants go to foreign countries to improve the lives of children, but what about the senior citizens in the good old United States. We have worked hard all of our lives and paid our taxes only to see American money going abroad in our declining years.

By this time our goals will be accomplished at Mingo Park. Our next step is to rent the ground floor (no steps) at the old dime store in downtown Delaware. The space will be needed to start our new consultant business. We will help, for a stiff fee, people or organizations that wish to:

Apply for Federal funding or grants.

Set up *PRESERVES* for animals, fauna or historical significance.

Make sure that seniors have their full constitutional rights protected in today's employment market.

OK, this is now a success story for three old gents, who were originally hired to pick up trash bags and clean restrooms. By the way, it should be mentioned that Phil was released from his duties at the Park for desertion. The Delaware County Fair was on and he found a better job seating people in the grandstand. The year was 1954 and he was a minor so those records have been expunged and stamped, "classified," to protect his lawful senior rights under the Constitution.

Phil Dunham, Ron Gabriel, Don Byerly

PAUL ORAHOOD

I met Paul when he and I carried Dispatch paper routes. I was a kid from the east side that wore glasses and Paul was from the north side. Somehow we struck up a friendship. Paul had a magnetic charisma about him. His blond hair and friendly smile attracted kids and made him popular. He always seemed to have a gang of kids around him.

He would invite me up to his house to play. There was always something going on. We would play war or cowboys and Indians. I remember the games would dissolve into huge shouting matches as to who was shot and who was suppose to be dead. One day we had a pickup football game in an empty lot behind Paul's house. I was amazed that Connie Jones and Kathleen Hayes got to play. That would never happen on my side of town. Except for Shirley Skatzes. She played football with us boys until one day her mother told her she was too old to play football with the boys. That was too bad because she was good and I always wanted her on my team. But back to Paul, Paul was the leader of the gang. He had all the ideas so everybody followed him. I met Phil Dunham through Paul, which has turned into a lifetime of close friendship.

I remember Paul and I going down old Route 23, playing along the Olentangy River behind the butcher shop where his dad worked. There was an old swinging bridge across the river. Paul had a 22 rifle and we went "frogging" along the marshy shores.

Although Paul and I were best buddies, it was a busy time. We had paper routes, Boy Scouts and I was in the church choir. This was the era of Junior High School and we were beginning to discover girls so Paul and I slowly drifted apart. About this time, Paul began hanging out downtown in the evening drinking coffee at the Hamburger Inn. He began to hang out with boys who's hair was too long, who wore denim jackets and black motorcycle boots with a black strap and a chrome buckle. Paul also dressed this way. In the language of the time, they were called hoods. A look of defiance was on their face but Paul still had that winning smile.

Much later in life Phil came back for a class reunion. We had heard that Paul was now bedridden. I phoned to see if he was accepting visitors. Rocky, his wife, said to come on out. The get together and conversations we had that day were bittersweet. It was good to see Paul again. His smile was still pure but life had dealt him a bad hand. He was optimistic and no words of self-pity were uttered. After we left, Phil said that was the best thing we could have done with our day. Later, I heard from Rocky that Paul was so excited about our visit that he was awake all night. After that day, I visited Paul many times but the day Phil and I drove the short six miles to Kilbourne to see Paul will remain with me forever. Kay Grandstaff Conklin, Connie Jones Maguire and others from our high school class made the pilgrimage to his bedside because Paul was in many of our enjoyable childhood memories.

Kay and I went to his funeral. It was a large gathering for someone who had been so isolated his last few years. His son and daughter got up and gave tearful testimonies to their father's life. But they never knew our Paul with whom we shared a wondrous childhood. Paul, thanks for the memories.

A GREAT BIKE ADVENTURE
ON THE
CHESAPEAKE AND OHIO CANAL

The preliminary planning

Somewhere, sometime, somehow I read an article on how Supreme Court Justice William O. Douglas saved the Chesapeake and Ohio Canal. The year was 1954 and a campaign was under way in Washington D.C. to construct a parkway to be modeled after the Skyline Drive over the old canal and towpath. The Washington Post had endorsed the idea. Justice Douglas wrote the Post, a now famous letter, challenging the newspaper to send reporters to hike the towpath with him. The newspaper accepted and on March 20, 1954, a group of people started on the old towpath near Cumberland, Maryland. Just a hand full of the ones that started, finished. The Washington Post reversed it's position, so a glimmer of hope started that the historic canal might be saved. It wasn't until 1972 that Richard Nixon signed a bill making the canal a National Park.

The dream of hiking the Chesapeake and Ohio Canal floated in and out of my mind for years. Last year Don Byerly and I had a rewarding experience returning to Sun Valley. The trip was a huge success. The return to our haunts of youth brought back many memories of our time spent there. After the trip, I wrote an account of what we did and felt while we were in Idaho. At the end, I wrote, "Next year the Chesapeake and Ohio Canal."

When Don and Eleanor came to Florida last winter, I tentatively brought the subject up. Both Joyce and Eleanor were wholeheartedly behind the idea. Don also was interested in the trip and thought it would be a lot of fun. Sometime, and I'm not sure when or how, the trip switched from hiking to bicycling. I think the deciding factor for me was the thought of sleeping on the ground. It just doesn't seem as much fun as it was when we were in Boy Scouts.

I already had a fifties type bicycle with big tires and a wide seat that I had stolen from Wal-Mart. Maybe I should explain. The bike was on special for around a hundred dollars. I told the clerk to put it back for me and I would go home and get *Brutus*, my big Dodge dually, diesel pickup truck. When I returned, the bike was sitting next to the building. I looked in the flower area for someone to pay. No clerk, so I got in my tool box and got a wrench to tighten the handlebars and the seat. I took a small ride and still no one was around the cash register to pay. I put the bike in the bed of the truck and went back into the store. No clerks were around. By this time, I was frustrated by the lack of proper service, so I jumped in Brutus and drove home. For two weeks I felt guilty and I began looking over my shoulder for *the coppers*. I finally went back to Wal-Mart and asked for the manager. I told him that I needed to pay for a bike. He said "Good, I will get someone for you." I said, "Don't bother I already have it at home." His eyes met mine and he immediately understood. He turned to the clerk and said, "Write up a bill for a bike. This gentlemen will tell you how much it is." He shook my hand, turned and walked away in a brisk managerial stride.

After returning from Florida in March, I stumbled onto the web site for the National Parks. From there I found the Chesapeake and Ohio Canal National Park. It is the longest, narrowest park in the country. The park runs from Cumberland, Maryland, 184.5 miles to Georgetown in the Washington, D.C. area. I ordered two books and some useless maps. The best book was Mike High's, "*The C & O Canal Companion*." This book contains the history, maps and very complete information on what to look for along the towpath and canal. The canal has mile markers, one being the start in Georgetown and marker 184 being near Cumberland. Also, the book has a list of motel and hotel addresses and phone numbers where you can stay as you bike the towpath. I began to map out the trip. Each night we would stay in a motel after a ride of around 25 to 30 miles. At eight miles an hour that would be only about five hours riding a day. This schedule would leave us plenty of time for rest stops and observing the scenery.

The information that I received did not say if the towpath was paved. In talking with different people that cycle, they felt that most of the path would be paved. Almost everyone I talked to had never heard of the C & O National Park. Even Mary Havens George and her husband, who have cycled all over the country, have not heard of the park. So on April 15th, I phoned the Cumberland, Maryland, visitor's center for the park and got a live person. Most of the time when phoning big business or big government, I get a recording. The answer voice says pleasantly, "If you want yada-yada, press one. If you want the weather, press two.

If you want to go to the bathroom, "hang up." On the first ring Rita answered and I said, "Rita are you a live person?" She replied, "The last time I checked." I liked her already, a person that serves the public and has a sense of humor. *I thought they went out with the hippies.* I told her about the trip on bicycles and asked her how much of the trail was paved. She said, "none!"

Don and I began these clandestine luncheons at Bun's where I would bring up my ideas and plans for riding the towpath in the fall. Don would smile knowingly between bites of steak. After one of these strategy luncheons, we moseyed over to the Breakaway Bike Shop. It was a sobering experience. They wanted $500 for a good bike and we would have to have three pairs of riding pants for the trip. One to wear, one to wash at the motel at night and dry the next day while we were riding. The third pair was in case it rained and the pair you were riding in got wet and the second pair you had washed, the night before, wasn't dry yet. Then you could slip on the third pair. One has to plan for everything, I guess. After much consternation, I decided that I could use "The Wal-Mart special" and I could ride in my regular Bermuda shorts.

The rest of April I spent taking small bike rides and reading "The C & O Canal Companion." About this time, I was thinking I would use a medium sized backpack for the trip. The plan was that we would drive our car over to Cumberland with the bike rack and two bikes. Then take the bike rack off and mail it to Washington D.C. When we were ready to leave Washington for home, we would rent a car and put the bike rack on it with the bikes and drive back to Cumberland.

I phoned cousin Sue Booe, who has taken many long bicycle trips. I feel she has complete knowledge of bikes and bike trips. Cousin Sue said, "no back packs," so back to the drawing board.

In June, Don purchased a slick new bicycle, a Giant Express with 21 gears and a carrier on the back. We took our bike ride through a housing development. The temperature was 83 degrees and it was very humid. The ride was a hot, sweaty affair. Don let me take a ride on his new bike. It was lightweight, easy to pedal and a smooth ride. The Wal-Mart special was not looking too good anymore.

I bought a new bike rack for the car on June 7th, we mounted the bikes on the rack for the first time and drove to the Delaware Dam area. It was a Saturday morning, so we thought the traffic in the park would be minimal. Wrong again, many boats and campers were going in and out of the park. At least the traffic was supposed to do twenty miles an hour. It rained some, but we estimated we rode six miles.

Our next ride was July 18th along the Olentangy River, from north of Worthington to the Ohio State Campus. It was another hot and humid day. The bike trail along the river was scenic and shaded as there were many large, mature trees. The area is mowed and the path is paved so it is like a long narrow park. Many people of all ages use the trail. There are cyclists, hikers, dog walkers, and rollerbladers. It was a good feeling to be outside with such a varied group of active people.

During the lunch break, at the Buckeye Hall of Fame Café, Don and I decided the best time to go on our adventure would be September 4^{th,} the day after Labor Day. We would spend six days riding the towpath which figures out to be twenty-five to thirty miles a day. On our way back north along the Olentangy, I notice how official Don looks. He has a white helmet with a white shirt and black gloves, with the end of the fingers cut off, and black bike pants. In fact, he has the air of a policeman. All he needs is a whistle, and I am still riding the Wal-Mart special with cut off jeans and an old Ohio State tee shirt. I let Don go in front to impress the on-comers. It was about this time that I decided I needed a new bicycle. On the way home, we went into the Breakaway Bike Shop and I told them, "I want a bike just like his."

On Sunday, July 22nd, I made the reservations for the trip. The first night after leaving Cumberland, we stay at Paw, Paw, West Virginia. The next night, Hancock, then Williamsport, Shepherdstown, Harper's Ferry, Leesburg, and then Washington D.C. for two nights at the Lombardy Hotel.

I picked up my new wonderful bike on August 1st. I also bought a red helmet, red gloves and a set of panniers, commonly know as saddle bags. Panniers sounds French. Words in the French language sound more refined, like faux pas (mistake,) mal de mare (sea sickness,) or derriere (your behind.) I feel like Rambo, wearing my red riding gloves with no fingers. It seems like I should pull out a big knife and threaten someone.

On August 31st, I went into the Breakaway Bike Shop and bought a patch tire kit, a tire pump and a tool set for the trip. Someone said we may need all that stuff.

I have received two e-mails. One from Mary Havens George in Florida. The Georges are avid bikers and are planning a trip to Santa Fe this fall. She is worried that I may get a sore behind. Phil Dunham's e-mail reflected the same warning. I have worried about different aspects of this adventure like, weather and my body conditioning, but my derriere has not been a priority worry.

Tuesday, September 4, 2001

On the first Tuesday after the first Monday in September, I put the rack and the bike on the car and drove over to pick up Don. In my day, school always started every year on the same date. The first Tuesday after the first Monday in September, the day after Labor day. School always let out before Memorial Day so that we could help with the crops and work in the fields.

We arrived in Cumberland, Maryland, at 2:30 pm and checked in at the Holiday Inn. They gave us permission to leave the car there for a week. We took the bike rack off the car and mailed it with some clothes to Washington D.C., where we will rent a car to drive back. The die is cast. Now we have to cycle to the Capitol. I have some misgivings. Are we in good enough condition? Can we do it? We have to try, I have told everybody I know about this bike ride, now I have to put up or shut up.

Cumberland is an old town with old brick homes and buildings that could use some repair. The old downtown area near the renovated train station must have had some federal restoration grants. A small two block area has been blocked off from traffic and a colonial brick walk or mall walkway has been constructed. The buildings in this area have been restored. It looks like the city fathers said, "We will get some federal money, fix this area up and people will flock back down to the old part of town." Wrong. Many of the renovated buildings are now empty. Right across the street from the Holiday Inn is a five story parking garage to handle all the cars that are not coming back to this neighborhood. The best laid plans sometimes just don't materialize.

The old train station houses the visitor's center for the Chesapeake and Ohio Canal National Park. It is also the start of the old towpath that runs 184.5 miles to Washington D.C. Tomorrow we start and I can hardly wait.

Wednesday, September 5, 2001

I was up super early. The hotel is located right by what has got to be the train capitol of the world. The trains rumbled in and out all night. I hung out in the lobby until Don got up. We took some pictures in front of the Visitor's Center then we started down the old towpath. It was a cool, damp morning and I was tired from listening to the trains all night. The first hour or two I was wondering what I had gotten myself into this time.

We passed a couple of guys on the trail. Their bikes were loaded down with camping gear. When we took a break, they would pass us and when they stopped we would pass them, so we hop scotched around each most of the day. One of the men was in his sixties and the other one in his thirties. We exchanged pleasantries each time we met. They were going to ride the trail in five days, camping out each night. They also provided us with valuable information on the trail, what to see and what to watch out for. In our haste to get on the trail we had forgotten lunch. We decided to have lunch in Old Town, Maryland.

In March of 1748, George Washington first came to Old Town. That was the first of many trips that he would make up the Potomac. Old Town was called Cresap at the time. Named after a crusty, vile fellow named Thomas Cresap. Washington was only sixteen at the time and he was with a surveying party laying out the boundaries of a land grant. From then until he died, in 1799, he was fascinated with the idea that the Potomac corridor could become a navigable water passage to Pittsburgh and the rich Ohio valley. This concept was the forerunner of the Chesapeake and Ohio Canal.

The little store in Old Town was on it's last legs. There was a, "FOR SALE," sign in front. Most of the items in the store, including food, looked like they had been there since the Nixon administration. We bought a sandwich, chips, and a pop. Across the road was a closed school building. We laid under a big shade tree and consumed our lunch. It was pleasant; a slight breeze blew the white clouds across a blue sky. We had ridden about nineteen miles this morning and have ten to go for a short afternoon.

The afternoon trail was a tree lined lane meandering through the woods with grass between the two wheel paths. The crystal clear Potomac was on our right and the old canal on our left as we peddled south. It is pristine, woodsy and scenic. With each turn we looked down the path in wonder. As the kids say, "It's awesome." Don and I talked on the way over about what type of country the path would be. Neither of us is disappointed. One of the cyclists we met called the towpath, "The longest dirt road he had ever seen."

The building of the Canal started in 1828 and was completed in 1850 when it reached Cumberland. The waterway would have been finished years sooner but the 3,171 foot Paw Paw Tunnel took years to build. When the Canal did reach Cumberland, it was outdated because the railroad had arrived in Cumberland in 1840.

After a 32 mile ride, we arrived in Paw Paw, West Virginia. The ride from the towpath to the bed and breakfast was around three miles, all up hill. The towpath is on the same level as the Potomac, so it's usually up hill when we leave the path for our night accommodations. A young policeman, dressed in jeans with a small gun and holster on his belt, directed us to our destination. He was driving an old Ford Bronco which fit in with the outfit.

The bed and breakfast was called, *The Paw Paw Patch*. It was an older two story residence. The inside was clean, neat and well decorated with comfortable furnishings. We stayed upstairs. There were three bedrooms, a bath and a large foyer at the top of the stairs. We were the only guests for the night so we had the bath to ourselves. The owners had a bedroom on the first floor.

It was around 3:30 in the afternoon when we arrived. We had seen a crane, four deer, ducks and a brown bear. Don claimed the latter was a cow. But it was all alone out in the middle of the canal, which was wider in that area, more like a bog. What would a lone cow be doing out there? I am sticking with my bear sighting. Besides, it makes for a better story. Who wants to hear about a cow sighting.

The woman of the house offered us iced tea and homegrown grapes. We sat in a wide, wooden swing in the back yard under a huge old shade tree. We discussed Ohio history, *John Adams*, the book by David McCullough, and parents relocating to be near the children and grandchildren. We both were tired from our first day on the trail. We went back to our room, took a shower and laid down. Since we did not want to get back on our bikes and find a restaurant, supper was a power bar and some cheese crackers in our room.

Thursday, September 6, 2001

We were served coffee, juice, pancakes and bacon for breakfast. The husband talked to us during breakfast. He said they have been open for cyclist for years. They have rented rooms to people from all over the world. The average age of their clientele was about fifty. He also informed us that the Paw Paw Tunnel was a real experience to go through and to be sure and stop at Little Orleans for lunch.

We entered the 3,171 foot Paw Paw Tunnel almost immediately after getting back on the trail the first thing in the morning. We were told by the park ranger in Cumberland to walk our bikes through the tunnel. It was very dark inside and seeing the stone walls and wood railings was difficult. We walked on the wooden deck-like structure where the mules used to pull the barges. Don and I both had flashlights but the farther we walked into the tunnel the darker it became. We could always see the light at both ends, but it seemed far away. When we got to the center, a feeling of disorientation came over us because objects could not be seen as clearly. It felt goofy and mildly alarming. After walking through the tunnel, one is impressed that such a monumental stone structure was built by hand in that era. A real engineering feat.

At the south end of the tunnel, we met a man and a boy that we would hop scotch with today. They were from Pittsburgh. The man had retired about a year ago and he was taking the neighbor's boy for an excursion on the towpath.

The bicycle ride was just as scenic today. A small lane meandering along the Potomac presented another inviting vista with each turn. The trail, shaded by large trees, seemed to go on forever. The Canal has been closed since 1924 so the trees have had 76 years to mature. Every hour or so we took a break and just sat in this cathedral of nature. It is difficult to fully experience the surroundings. Society has cultured us to be in constant motion and to have some type of sound bombarding our senses at all times; radio, television, talking, cars, planes, anything but stillness. I think we have forgotten the eloquence of silence. In one of our many breaks, we wandered down to the Potomac and skipped flat stones across the water.

We stopped for lunch at a little town close to the trail called Little Orleans. A 79 year old man with a cigar and an attitude ran the restaurant/bar type establishment. The original building burned down a year or so ago. He built the new building and kept on working. It is what he wants to do with his life. The first thing when we walked in the door, Bill (the owner) said, "Just sandwiches, nothing off the grill." A sign hanging on the wall in the corner said;

"THIS IS NOT BURGER KING
YOU GET THE SON OF A BITCH
OUR WAY OR NOT AT ALL.
THE MANAGEMENT"

We chatted with the fellow we met on the trail from Pittsburgh during lunch. He has ridden on the Erie Canal towpath in upper New York State. He told us about the Rails to Trails path that runs from Pittsburgh south for a little over one hundred miles. It is projected that in years to come this trail will meet up with the Chesapeake and Ohio Canal towpath which would then connect Pittsburgh and Washington D. C. with a recreational trail.

In the late afternoon, we rode our bikes into downtown Hancock, Maryland. Hancock is a clean, old fashioned, small town that was created by the canal years ago. There is an extensive renewal program going on in the downtown area. There is a new brick sidewalk and some of the building fronts have been restored. We found out our motel was ten blocks back the other way so we were riding back down the sidewalk towards our lodging, as two young boys came up to me, one was a towhead with no shirt and the other was taller with a lock of unruly dark hair. They looked ornery in a nice way. They reminded me of a modern day Tom Sawyer and Huck Finn. The towhead said, "Mister, did you know that you ain't allowed to ride you're bike on the sidewalk." Then the other one said, "Yeah, the cops took my bike." I told them that we had been riding these bikes for thirty-five miles today, we were tired and if the cops wanted the bikes, they could have them.

After checking into the motel, we showered, napped and then walked down to a local restaurant called, *Weavers*. We had a delicious meal to top off a great day on the towpath.

Friday, September 7, 2001

There was a boisterous group of people in the motel dining area for the free continental breakfast. They were all in their mid-forties or fifties and they were also riding the canal trail like we were. We talked with a friendly couple from Australia. Upon leaving the motel, we stopped at a supermarket to buy some bottled water. We talked to a couple who advised us to use the Rails to Trails paved bike path that runs parallel to the C & O Canal for about ten miles. At first, I thought I wanted to be a purist and stay on the historic towpath. Then I though how easy the pedaling would be. Don agreed. The first ten miles of the day went by like coasting down hill.

After about two hours back on the towpath, all outside thoughts slipped from my mind. I began to absorb this gorgeous scenic country. The only thoughts on my mind were today, this hour, this minute and this trail. It was like a Zen experience. The methodic pedaling was the mantra and this time like nirvana. Later on, we were riding quietly, when Don said out loud to no one in particular, "Seize the day." We must have been experiencing the same emotions.

We stopped at Fort Frederick for lunch. It was about a mile off the trail. The fort was built of stone in the early 1800's. The Civilian Conservation Corps restored the fort in the 1930s. We were the only ones there except for some gnats, with whom we shared our lunch.

We met four other people on the trail today. A real crowd. Everyone that we encountered was friendly. We usually stop and converse. We have learned some valuable information from these little chats. We made good time today and arrived at the visitor's center in Williamsport at 2:30 pm. The motel was up hill and across town. After checking in, we went across the street to McDonalds and bought a snack. We were back in civilization. There was a large, cool looking swimming pool outside our room. It had been a hot day on the towpath so a cool dip in the pool sounded refreshing.

Williamsport is where General Lee limped back to the Potomac after Gettysburg. When he got there, the river was high and he had to wait five days for it to subside. In the mean time, Meade came leisurely marching down from the north. When he arrived there, he had his men dig fortifications around Williamsport and the confederates. Once the work was done, Meade decided to wait one more day before engaging Lee's army. Meade hoped to pin the rebel army against the Potomac. The day Meade finally decided to engage his troops, he found that the whole army of northern Virginia had slipped across the river in the night. Lincoln was furious, Meade lost his command and Grant was sent for because he had just won Vicksburg, a decisive battle in the West.

Saturday, September 8, 2001

The towpath was busier today. Many riders were taking advantage of a beautiful September weekend. We were detoured off the towpath onto some hilly Maryland roads. We had not realized how lucky we had it on the flat towpath. The hills were real killers. Our 21 gear bikes helped a little but it was grueling. In fact, hill is now a swear word for me, I wince when I say it.

When it gets hot and humid, like on the detour, I keep cool by wearing a big, blue farmer's handkerchief around my neck. It looks like a bandana worn in old western movies. The villains would pull the bandana up over their nose and say, "Stick 'um up," when they robbed a stagecoach. Their next line usually was, "Throw down the strong box."

Every three to five miles along the towpath there is a primitive campground. Each has a couple of picnic tables, an old fashioned water pump and usually a gorgeous view of the Potomac. There is also a porta-potty at each campground. I don't like these little metal monsters. Man has gone in the woods for centuries, it's our historic link to the past. I guess it must be a male thing.

Along towards the middle of the afternoon, we were taking a break; usually, we lay down on the ground or on a picnic table to rest. I told Don that I could hear drums. It sounded like drums in a marching band doing a street beat. Don just looked at me. He informed me that I have had one bear sighting and now drums in the woods. He thinks that all this quiet outdoor nature environment is getting to me. About fifteen minutes later, we rode up a huge hill and across a very high bridge into Shepherdstown, West Virginia. As we gruelingly pumped our way up the hill to the Bavarian Inn, we could hear a crowd yelling from a football game. Come to find out, Shepherd College is located here and they were having a home football game on a pleasant, autumn Saturday afternoon. There was even a band playing to arouse school spirit. Between the band's musical selections, drums could be distinguished. You know, I still think that was a bear I saw. I may start looking for Elvis.

The Bavarian Inn is located on a hill with a spectacular view of the Potomac and the hills beyond. We had a plush room with a deck overlooking the river. The well-decorated room had two big beds, a matching couch and chair, and a stylish desk in the corner. The wallpaper was even impressive. We showered, laid on the beds and watched some college football. The announcer said Ohio State won their football game 27 to 7. *All is right with the world.* We felt almost human again.

To eat in the main dining room, one must have a shirt with a collar and long pants. I had neither. Don claimed to have an outfit like that in his saddlebags. He has been pulling amazing things out of those saddlebags since we left Cumberland. He even has this huge book on John Adams. My saddlebags are filling up with dirty laundry. I may have to start wearing clothes over again. So I have informed Don that if we get some funny looks on the trail, just ignore them.

We did get to eat in the lower level. I had the best piece of prime rib that I have had in years. Don ordered a couple of things that I couldn't pronounce and an ice cream type dessert that looked like a picture from a cooking magazine. After a long leisurely meal that took us close to two hours, we walked around the well landscaped grounds. The buildings are all designed with a Bavarian motif. There was a large wooden deck with comfortable chairs where the guests have a panoramic view of the Potomac and the green tree lined, *Endless Mountains*, as the Indians called them.

Sunday, September 9, 2001

I woke up early and watched out the window as it began to get light. The colors in the eastern sky, silhouetted by the mountains, turned from night to a rose glow, then red. As the light increased, a yellow beam of sun shot out from over the far mountains. This beam of light announced a new day for our enjoyment.

We ate breakfast in the main dining room this morning. The food and service were excellent. The Bavarian Inn is one of the nicest places

I have stayed. The décor is elegant, the rooms plush, the facility is architecturally pleasing, the views spectacular, the employees extremely friendly and the water is excellent. The best I have ever drank.

We rode our bikes into downtown Shepherdstown. The colonial brick reflects the town's age and history. The downtown was busy; there was a farmer's market and a dulcimer festival going on. We came back to the room to rest before checking out. Yesterday we navigated the killer detour in Maryland and it was no little accomplishment to get up to Shepherdstown from the towpath, so our tired bodies are talking back to us. Harper's Ferry, our next stop, is only twelve miles so it should be a short day. We begrudgingly left the Bavarian Inn around 11:00 am. We coasted two miles back down to the canal for the day's journey.

The Potomac and the towpath were very busy today. Families were out enjoying some Sunday recreation and many bright colored kayaks dodged the many outcropping of rocks in the river. The Potomac has been getting wider as we make our way south.

We arrived across the river from Harper's Ferry around 1:00 pm. A railroad line crosses the Potomac on an old bridge that looks like it was built before the Civil War. The Shenandoah River flows into the Potomac at Harper's Ferry. The Shenandoah separates the states of West Virginia and Virginia. To get to Harper's Ferry we had to carry our bikes up metal spiral stairs attached to the railroad bridge. There were many historical buildings and even an ice cream shop in downtown Harper's Ferry, but we rode on through in our quest to get to our lodging for the night. We made a wrong turn and had to go up this almost insurmountable hill. It took us an hour and we were low on water on a hot day. We tried to tell ourselves that much later this is going to make a good story. After we arrived on the summit of the hill, we coasted back down to the motel which was very close to where we started.

We arrived at the motel at 2:30 pm and were completely worn out. We showered, had a large greasy pizza delivered, then flaked out and watched football. I phoned the front desk and asked them if they did laundry. She said a large commercial load cost $6.38. I told her to come and get it. Don and I got all our dirty laundry ready. All the laundry would go in one load. I even took the clothes off that I was wearing. When she came back with the clean laundry, I modestly stood behind the door and reached my hand out.

Monday, September 10, 2001

We left the motel and rode uphill for four blocks, then turned and coasted the mile to the center of town. We went into one of the historic buildings and viewed some pictures of John Brown, who was hung here in the late 1850s. Then we headed across the river, back down the metal spiral stairs and onto the towpath. The Appalachian Trail and the Chesapeake and Ohio Canal use the same path, south of Harper's Ferry, for about six miles. We encountered a girl coming up the trail. She had a backpack, sturdy shoes and clothes. I asked her if she was hiking the Appalachian Trail. She said yes, then she told us she was hiking half the trail this year and hopefully the other half next year. I thought how lucky she was to be hiking down the Shenandoah Valley into the Great Smoky Mountains in the fall.

We crossed the Potomac on a ferry at White's Ford. The Potomac is wide here so it was a scenic ride. After we crossed the Potomac we had a five mile ride on a busy highway into Leesburg, Virginia. As we methodically pedaled our bikes toward Leesburg, we could see rain clouds moving swiftly in from the west. The wind increased and blew the fall leaves as we hurriedly pumped our way through the center of Leesburg. We approached our day's end at the Days Inn Motel, as raindrops sporadically descended. Just as we pushed our bikes into the motel, it began to rain heavily. We had ridden 32 miles.

I seem to be leaving things at motels. The trip schedule was left in Cumberland, our maps at Paw Paw, the shampoo in Hancock and so on. By the time we get to Washington, I should have much less of a load to pack for the trip home.

September 11, 2001

It was a sunny Tuesday morning. We had decided to take the Washington and Old Dominion Rails to Trails Bike Path into Washington D.C. The trail was more convenient because it was located a block behind our motel. The towpath was five miles way. Yesterday the C & O towpath had been muddy is some spots. The bike trail was paved and ran through open Virginia countryside so there were no trees and it was hotter than the towpath. The riders on the bike path were not as friendly as they were on the C & O. Most of the cyclists whizzed by us like they were in training for the world championship. They did not even nod as they flew by.

We rode about eight miles an hour. A nice pace. I have an odometer that has around fourteen functions. It has a small two-inch screen. When I had it put on my bike in Delaware, they set it to show the mileage. It came with a big instruction booklet that explained all the functions, but I don't read instructions; they mix me up. Don has a compass on his bike. He yells over to me and asks, "How fast are we going?" After I tell him, I ask "What direction are we headed?" These exchanges make for good conversation when we run out of things to say. Don also has a bell on his bike that he rings when we are going to pass someone. We have passed about two people in six days on the trail. Not to be outdone, I have a water bottle attached to the frame and some shiny new wrenches. But Don has this really slick canvas water bag that straps to his back with a tube up over his shoulder so he can drink from it anytime without using his hands. Very impressive. I can't seem to keep up with him with all the technology and luxuries, but I am seriously thinking of having a global positioning system installed.

One of the inconveniences we noticed on the Rails to Trails this morning, was the busy crossroads. We had to stop and walk our bikes across the streets or highways. When we were on the C & O towpath, it was next to the Potomac and any road crossings over the Potomac from West Virginia, Virginia and to Maryland were on high bridges that also spanned the towpath and canal. This meant we had very few, "at grade crossings," as we say in the Ohio Department of Transportation lingo.

We started on the bike path about 9:00 am and we pedaled into Herndon, Virginia, around 10:45 am. There was a restored old railroad caboose along the bike path in the center of town. We stopped for some pictures. The morning ride had been around fifteen miles. We had just spotted a Dairy Queen when a policeman came walking by. I asked him how far it was to Washington D.C. He said, "You don't want to go there!" Then he told us about the horrendous things that happened that morning in New York and Washington. We just starred at him. It was hard to believe the words coming out of his mouth. We sat dazed in front of the Dairy Queen not knowing what to do. Herndon, Virginia, is where Dullas Airport is located, so the whole town was in shock. A man that worked in an insurance agency stopped and talked to us. He volunteered to take us to a car rental agency. We rented an enclosed 17 foot truck so we could transport our bikes. The truck looked just like what a terrorist would use to transport bombs. We drove the truck back and loaded our bikes. The first hour on the road, we hit some heavy Washington D.C. traffic. We arrived in Cumberland around 3:00 pm, picked up my car and kept on rolling.

Supper was in Morgantown, West Virginia, at Bob Evans. During supper, I was expounding on what I would do to those terrorists, then I went right straight into a long dissertation on the bad meal I had just received and how in the old days people took more pride in their work. I was just about half way through my opinion on ill-mannered truck drivers when I looked over and Don was just nodding and smiling. It took me back fifty years when cousin Sara Hanlon said, "Ace (Don's nick name when he was younger) just smiles all the time." Ace has been listening to me for fifty-some years. The sun is still setting and the moon is still rising. Some things will never change.

After supper, Don pulled out in the rental "terrorist" truck, leading the way home. A little east of New Concord, Ohio, I thought a helicopter was flying over me. I could hear a loud thump-thump. Then I realized it was a tire on my car. I pulled off the inter-state. Don was way ahead by now with no way to contact him. I drove by a couple of gas stations. They were packed with cars and trucks filling up with fuel. There was a rumor that gas was going to $4.50 a gallon. I stopped across from a BP station next to the interstate. The guy at the cash register told me he had been on duty since 3:00 pm and he had not been able to leave the register.

I phoned Joyce and we discussed the options. Then I phoned AAA. He was there in ten minutes. With AAA, I could get towed for three miles free. From there on, it was twenty cents a mile. If I had a gold card, I would have unlimited towing. Guess who didn't have a gold card. The young guy from AAA was nice, he told me that if I was towed very far, the cost would be more than a new set of tires. He advised me that if he put on the little donut spare tire and I drove 55 miles an hour, I could make it 100 miles. I looked up at the sign next to the inter-state it said Columbus 69 miles. It would be another 24 to Delaware. Lets see, that would be 93 miles. So I said, "put it on." I filled up with cheap gas; now, any gas less then $4.50 is cheap. It was 9:30 pm so I phoned Joyce and asked her to meet me at the Wal-Mart on SR 23 south of Delaware at 11:30 pm. I was going to leave the car at Wal-Mart and have a new set of tires put on. I turned my trouble blinker lights on and pulled onto the inter-state at 50 miles per hour. I didn't want to listen to the radio and hear more about the plane crashes so I turned off the radio and sang loudly all the way home. The trucks and other vehicles seemed to respect my trouble lights which made the trip smoother. On the way home, I realized that I still had a decent voice. Only, I wished that I knew more of the words to the songs. Don told me once that I was the only one he knew that improvised on the lyrics and the melodies. I'm not sure if that was a compliment.

I pulled into Wal-Mart right on time, parked by the Tire Department, grabbed my saddlebags and walked around to the front of the store to wait for Joyce. After ten minutes, I was getting a little chilly. I began to wonder if Joyce went to the wrong Wal-Mart. There is a Super Wal-Mart ten miles down the road. What a day, I was getting cold and tired. Just about the time I was ready to go into a panic mode, Brutus, our Dodge diesel pickup, appeared on the horizon like the cavalry. Joyce was behind the wheel and Tad, the wonder dog, was peering out the passenger side window. *I was home!*

A LOST FRIEND

On a balmy April evening, my life was jolted by a phone call from Idaho. An old friend had died. It had happened in November, six months earlier. It seemed almost too late to grieve.

My friend and I had loafed together, drank and chased girls together and drove old cars too fast, over desolate Idaho roads in the late fifties.

We had seen each other just three fleeting times since I left those rugged mountains in 1961. But there was always that deep bond that one only has with true friends. Time and distance does not disconnect. We always took up right where we left off.

My friend was short and stocky with the shoulders and arms of a body builder. When we were out raising hell in the local western bars, no one would mess with us because of his presence and reputation. Even though he didn't show it, he was really good-natured and if he liked you it was forever.

He was the cement that held our little gang of misfits together. He chose us to be part of the group and we felt honored to be selected and receive his friendship. The close knit group worked in the Sun Valley commissary. Our life was dedicated to having fun which wasn't hard to do in that free and innocent time.

The Sawtooth Mountains were a great place to be in the late fifties. It was pristine, sparsely populated with spectacular scenery everywhere. We had small motorcycles that we used to explore old mountain roads and trails. Our searches for excitement led us down lonely highways at ninety miles an hour while downing six packs of Olympia beer.

Thinking back over the past forty years to that wonderful time of youth, the memories of him, the laughter, and the good times we shared has a special place in my heart. It is hard now to define why it happened. We came together, had fun and then life pushed us down different highways. Now he is gone and I can't return to share with him the memories of our time together.

FINGER FOOD

Corn-on-the-cob is in season now here in Ohio. Just smear some butter on it and sprinkle salt and pepper, then eat it with your hands. *Boy, is it tasty*! You know it's summer when roasted ears appear at the table.

Certain foods have a small window of opportunity. The big plump turkey we eat just once a year at Thanksgiving. Pumpkin pie is limited to autumn and strawberry shortcake to early June. The reason used to be that this was when the crops were harvested. But now, with the big freezer in the basement, these foods can be eaten anytime. Watermelon would be the exception. I have never seen anybody freeze a piece of watermelon still on the rind. There is nothing that makes food taste any fresher or better than when it is just picked from the tree or pulled from the garden.

I have to say that one thing that enhances the flavor of food considerably is when it's eaten with the hands. Corn-on-the-cob for instance, you just grab it with your fingers and start eating. It actually adds to the flavor of the corn. You can take a chicken leg and cut it with a knife, then turn the fork around and poke the piece of chicken, and then lift it daintily to your mouth, but the real joy of eating a chicken leg is to pick it up with your fingers and chomp on it. There is a ton of flavor lost when a knife and fork are used. When using the hand technique, no flavor is lost because you always have the option of licking your fingers. Have you ever heard of licking a fork?

There is a special thing I do in the fall after a big meal. I slip into the kitchen, where there is always a piece of pumpkin pie left over. I stealthily pick up a piece in my hand and eat it on the go. It tastes better even though it doesn't have the dab of whipped cream on the top. This process cuts down on the formality of getting a small plate out, searching for a clean fork and taking it to the living room where they would make fun of me for having another piece of pie. When eaten in the kitchen by hand sometimes no one knows.

I have observed a couple of truths about holiday meals. The first, is when a large family eats at one table and there are a lot of dishes that must be passed around before you are supposed to start eating. There is always someone who tries to sneak a quick fork full of food. The second, is when the dish or dishes come back around, the table has shrunk. There's no room on the table for the returning dishes. Where did the space go? The spot the dish vacated was just there before you started passing them around.

Some people will not touch a leftover. It's a matter of pride with them. Personally, I think the food tastes better when left to set and the different ingredients permeate. A late night snack using your God given fingers on Thanksgiving or Christmas can turn out to be one of the most scrumptious meals of the year.

There are many rules of etiquette about what, when, and how to eat, but some of my fondest memories are of times sitting around the table eating with family and friends. That's when I want to have just one more dab of this or that before the food is whisked off to the kitchen to be sealed in plastic and hidden in the refrigerator where I can never find it.

SHOWERS

We used to take a bath once a week in an old tub in the middle of the kitchen floor. We all used the same water. This event took place on Saturday night because Church was on Sunday.

With the advent of bathrooms and showers, bathing has become an easier event.

How often we take showers is a personal decision but society frowns on those who don't shower often enough. Some people are very proud of when and how often they shower. Their conversations are sprinkled with references to their showering practices. Maybe they are hinting at me?

I used to work for an old engineer on the survey crew who claimed that bathing too often took much needed natural oils out of the skin. I think he felt the same way about his clothes. He was from the old school, a hard worker and everything had to be just right. So, should we question him?

Hardly anyone takes a bath anymore. The last bath I took was a decade ago.

The haunting question facing society now is, "Do you shower the last thing at night or first thing in the morning?" One wants to always be clean but if you took your shower at night and wanted to go out to dinner the next evening, it would have been at least eighteen hours since your last shower. Could you really, in the name of good hygiene, go out to dinner without taking another shower?

I wonder if someone can really be a good person if they are unclean or smell? I shutter to think what the old cowboys were like after being on the trail for three months. *PHEW!* Or what about our ancestors, who were sewn into their long underwear for the winter? *DOUBLE PHEW!*

Now, this diatribe will not change your shower habits, but you should realize that society places boundaries on us that we may not be aware of unless pointed out by a decorated self-appointed member of the shower patrol.

BATH TOWELS

I would like to address the age old question of how often to change the bath towel after a shower.

Richie (no one you know) uses three bath towels when he showers. I won't go into why three and where he uses those three. It would be a tasteless discussion. Richie uses those bath towels just once. He then discards them into the dirty towel hamper.

The other side of the coin is the person who reuses their bath towel over and over again. They claim that the body is clean after a shower so the towel is drying off clean water.

Now the reader will probably want me to take a stand on this bath towel issue. I refuse to be drawn into such an emotion-laden subject. It is a personal thing and up to the reader to make up his or her own mind. If you feel that you need support for your opinion, Google it. Google has an answer for everything. If you are still in search of a more definitive answer, write *Dear Abby*.

Common sense would reveal to us that the great bath towel question would be at the bottom of our major concerns in life. Although the issue comes up every day, until now, you weren't aware of the debate.

After this discussion you can no longer have the luxury of ignoring this issue. It is your hygienic duty to at least think about it and maybe take some half-hearted stand.

Remember, cleanliness is next to Godliness. Who said that? Was it Ben Franklin, Mark Twain or the makers of Lava soap?

MY MORNING RITUAL

After rising in the morning, I brew my coffee, drink my orange juice and then I sit in a dazed state and drink coffee until I am fully awake.

Next, I get dressed and put on my tennis shoes. I refuse to call them sneakers. A walk is next on the schedule. My morning stroll takes me within half a block of a grade school. If I am running a little late, recess is in progress. I can hear the spontaneous giggles, shouts, and the uproar of innocent little kids having fun being alive. These uplifting sounds can put a smile on your face. If you ever get depressed, Doctor Gabriel recommends that you stand by a grade school playground at recess. If someone official comes up and asks you what you're doing, don't mention Doctor Gabriel.

My walk is about a mile and ends at Buehlers. Buehlers is a super duper grocery with a restaurant, Ace Hardware store and a bakery. This one building solves all of man's wants and needs. Seniors hang out there in the morning so the store also serves as a stop and chat community senior center.

As I come ambling across the parking lot, I observe the time and temperature posted on the outside of the building. This current weather information I report to the women behind the bakery counter. The staff is breathlessly awaiting my report because they have been on duty since 7:00 am. They are not aware of the current outside weather conditions. Sometimes they try to act indifferently to my weather report but down deep I know they can hardly wait to hear it.

After my "Weather Man" duties, I help myself to a FREE donut sample that is on the counter for the paying customers. While munching on the FREE piece of donut, I amble over to the donation coffee counter. This is where I get a cup of coffee for a small offering. I usually put in a quarter and consider myself generous. Some mornings I refuse to drink some of their coffee flavors like: German Chocolate Cake, Raspberry Chocolate, Chocolate Marshmallow, French Roast, French Vanilla. I don't like anything that has French attached to it. I consider these flavors to be too feminine. They should have more masculine flavors like: Rawhide, Camp Fire Blend, Trail Herd Leavings or He Man's Brew.

The next stop is the magazine rack where the store has provided benches for those waiting for a prescription to be filled from the Pharmacy. The benches are a perfect place for me to sip my coffee and peruse the latest sports magazines. This up-dates me on whatever of importance is going on in the sporting world.

Upon leaving the store, I walk by the area where the groceries are being loaded into the customer's car by a store employee. The employee on duty is a contemporary of mine which is a nice way of saying he is in my age bracket. His name is Charlie and we are both avid Ohio State football fans. We opinionize not only the present Buckeye situation but we have been known to go as far back as to the All American abilities of Vic Janowicz. Our exchanges are brief while he is loading the groceries but they are profound and pleasurable.

I take the short cut back home, on the bike path, over the wooden bridge by the flock of ducks near the pond and across the yard down into Bennington Cove to home. Now I can begin another day of activities, of my own choosing, in my retirement.

AN OHIO STATE FAN

When I gaze into the mirror, I wonder if I need a guardian appointed to watch over me. The mirror reflects a grown man with an Ohio State hat, a red Ohio State shirt, wide, red, strap suspenders with the large letters, *O S U*, on each strap, white socks with bright colored Ohio State emblems and even an Ohio State watch to tell me what time it is in Buckeye Nation. I am sipping coffee out of an OSU cup that has four students spelling, *O-H-I-O*, with their arms in the air. This picture in the mirror is the culmination of decades of Ohio State fandom.

My first visit to the *Horseshoe* was in the fall of 1949. For those who aren't lucky enough to be a Buckeye fan, *The Shoe* is Ohio State's mammoth football stadium. As a boy scout in Troop 93, I volunteered to seat fans at Ohio State home football games.

The crowd always flooded into my section to be directed to their reserved seats just as the marching band came out of the tunnel in the closed end of the field. I was only able to get glimpses of the pageantry of this pre-game activity.

There was more drinking in the stands in those days. Beer bottles were tossed over the back of the stadium. Fans would buy a coke, drink some and then fill it with booze. The smell of whisky was in the air. I can remember one guy in the third quarter braying loudly "Get the ball, get the ball." It didn't matter who had the ball.

Right after the first half of the game, the announcer would say something like, "The attendance today is 83,474. It is the third largest crowd ever in the stadium." Everyone would clap and yell to be a part of the history and tradition of the great stadium. Now, *The Shoe* holds 105,000 fans.

Vic Janowicz was the star player of the 1949 season. In 1950, he won the Heisman Trophy that is given to the best college football player in the country. Of all the All Americans that Ohio State has ever had, Vic, number 31, is my favorite. He did everything. He played offense and defense, punted, kicked field goals, ran the ball and caught passes. He was the complete package. Now the players are specialized; offense, defense, running back, wide receiver etc.

Vic fit the mold of football players of that era. He played hard, partied hard and enjoyed the campus coeds and bars. I would remind you that this era was soon after World War II. The boys from the war were going to school on the G I Bill, which means the government was paying. These boys (or men) had seen it all and they liked to have fun by downing some cold brews.

Now, the players train year around. If the football players get caught playing "boys will be boys," some attention-seeking reporter will get the scandal in print or on television. Back then, if old number 31 got in trouble for extra curricular activities, it was hushed up and the game went on.

In Vic's senior year, Woody Hayes switched him to wide receiver. Vic didn't like this so he and Woody feuded all through the season. After the last game of the year (Michigan), Vic did not ride home with the team.

There will always be only one Woody Hayes and he will never be forgotten. I can still picture him in a white, short sleeve shirt in November, standing on the sidelines on cold, snowy, Saturday afternoons yelling at the players to give their best.

For me, there has been no greater spectacle as on a fall Saturday afternoon when, *The Best Damn Band in the Land*, emerges onto the field from the north tunnel at *The Shoe*. The drum major leads the band through the script Ohio and then the National Anthem. If that doesn't bring a lump to your throat or a tear to your eye, you're not a true Buckeye. Then the team comes running out in their vivid scarlet and gray uniforms onto the deep green field. The cheerleaders precede the team carrying huge *Ohio State* banners. The crowd of 105,000 jumps to their feet yelling their approval and appreciation as the team thunders onto the field. It's been sixty-five years since I witnessed my first Ohio State game and it never gets old.

As I walk away from the mirror with my game attire in place, all is right with the world. It's another colorful fall in Ohio and better yet, it's game day.

GO BUCKS!

PERSONAL BEST

Someone once said that an unexamined life is not worth living. When examining my life to see what I have accomplished of some importance, I have always been fearful of viewing my life and thoughts in the true light of day. I think I am mentally sound, but if I told people why I do what I do or my decision making process, they would have deep reservations about my mental stability.

All this is leading up to a particular feat that I accomplished. Most people would not be the least bit impressed, but each of us has individual deeds that we are proud of and we hold sacred to our very being.

In the fall of 2010, on a Saturday, I ensconced myself in my comfortable recliner at 11:45 am. I proceeded to watch college football until 11:15 pm. A total of eleven hours and thirty minutes straight with only potty, coffee, pop, and pumpkin pie breaks. This is my personal best for length of time watching football.

I have been in training for this achievement for more years than I would care to admit. I would like to think that training and practice was my highway to this achievement. This deed of mine is really a gift that one must be born with. It comes down to whether you have it or you don't.

This accomplishment catapults me into a small group of true sportsmen that have sacrificed for a good cause. From here on, I feel that my *uncriticizable* opinion should be given credence over less dedicated men. When I speak, a hush should come over the room and women should lower their eyes when I pass by.

So you say, what is left for me in life? Do I try to better my already miraculous achievement? Do I sit back and enjoy the adulation? Maybe it is enough for me to know in my inner being, I have stepped up to the plate and hit a home run.

Erma Bombeck once said, "If a man can watch three football games in a row, he should be pronounced brain dead." My answer to that is, "Duh."

SPORTS IN OUR TIME

The Super Bowl is being played in February this year. Football in February, can you believe it? Football in the middle of winter!

The seasons for different sports are getting to be way too long. One sports season runs into another so that two sports are running concurrently. The present scheduling upsets my already fragile focus. I cannot give each sport it's just due.

My plan is to change the whole yearly seasonal scheduling for sports. In my plan, the baseball season would last from Memorial Day to Labor Day with the All-Star game being played the Fourth of July. The World Series would be played over the Labor Day weekend.

Football season would start the first Saturday after Labor Day for both college and professional teams, and last until New Year's Day.

Basketball season would start the day after New Year's and be completed the first weekend in April.

As long as I am changing the sports' scene, I think that, *The Star Spangled Banner*, should not be played before every sporting event. It takes away from the special patriotic nature of the National Anthem. This piece, which is a national treasure, should be played every Sunday at our National Veterans Cemeteries. To do it up right, *Taps*, should also be played at dusk. The veterans deserve it. If you want my opinion, *America the Beautiful*, should be our National Anthem. If they want to sing something before ball games, sing, *Take Me Out to the Ball Game*. It's a fun tune and it makes you feel good to sing it along with the other fans at *the old ball game*.

There is nothing for me to watch, sports-wise, on television between the NCAA college basketball tournament final, *March Madness,* and the first wonderful Saturday of the collegiate football season in September. For some reason I'm not a baseball fan; not that there's anything wrong with baseball. This period of time is long and tedious for me.

It is during this time that I get out my videotapes of Ohio State football games. I review the games OSU won. I don't watch the ones they lost. The tapes help me to get through the great vacuum that exists during the bleak summer of sports on television.

I do not watch professional football, basketball or baseball. I think the players are extremely overpaid and I don't want to contribute to their, *overpaidness*. After all is said and done, they are grown men playing a boys' game.

College sports players get what is called a full-ride scholarship. The scholarship pays for school, books and food. The collegiate coaches make huge amounts of money and the universities make millions off these gifted athletes. I believe that if the sport the student athlete plays, makes money for the university, the athlete should be given a stipend for their personal expenses. I am thinking in the range of $50.00 a week.

If my plan is adopted, pro players would make less money because of fewer games. This would mean that the big money the television broadcasting companies shower on the owners of the pro teams would be curtailed.

Due to the overriding pursuit of money by the owners and professional athletes, the season for sports has been stretched to play more games and make even more money.

The world has turned upside down when a lineman or a football team makes ten times what the president of the United States makes. Of course, the lineman doesn't get his own airplane or his own White House.

My advice to you is to go ahead and enjoy football in February, baseball in late October and basketball in July because my logical, reasonable proposal is just not going to be adopted in our lifetime.

DO OVERS

If I could have "do over's" for my life, what would I change?

One thing, I would be nicer to my wonderful mother. She was the biggest influence in my life and a warm, giving woman who loved to entertain in her home. She loved me unconditionally which meant she forgave me for all the bratty things I said and did.

I would read all the directions for assembling things before trying to put them together. I have never liked to read directions because, for me, they are more trouble than helpful.

I would learn to cook.

I would floss more.

I would listen more to my sister, Sally, about music. She appreciated the jazz greats at a young age. It has taken me seventy years to get to where she was, musically, as a young woman.

I would give more money to those Santa's who ring their bells at Christmas. They stand out in the cold for what they believe in. Not too many people do that any more.

I would try harder to finish that workbook assignment given to me by my fifth grade teacher, Mrs. Warren.

I would take better care of my first car, then maybe it would have lasted longer.

I would work harder to become an Eagle Scout. I had more than enough merit badges to be a Life Scout and I only needed a few more to get the Eagle Scout award.

I would try to get Vic Janowicz's autograph. He was my favorite Ohio State Heisman trophy winner of all time.

I would not buy a television remote control which means I would have to get up each time I wanted to change the channel. This would stop my two hours a day of channel flipping to find out afterwards that there is nothing on the tube that I am interested in.

I would ask my aunts where my great-grandmother Anne Williams Owens was buried.

I would definitely write more thank you notes.

I would ask out that beautiful Japanese girl who worked in the Japanese Tea Garden in Golden Gate Park in San Francisco. The year was 1959.

I would tell Pudge Ward, a grade school classmate, that he was a bully.

I would not drop out of Miss Bussard's Spanish 2 class under the lame excuse that I would never need to know Spanish.

I would collect all the baseball cards I could get my hands on.

We don't get any *do over's* in this life, but we do get a lot of second chances if we are smart enough to take them.

GRANDPARENTING

I became a grandparent late in life. I was almost sixty-eight when Ian was born and sixty-nine when Grace appeared. By this time, I had given up on the likelihood of being a grandparent.

Life without grandchildren didn't bother me much because some of the grandparents I knew had completely lost it. The front of their refrigerators were covered with pictures of their grandchildren along with goofy crayon drawings that had colors that didn't stay in the lines.

The new grandparents changed overnight to picture-showing, story-telling bores. They had to see the grandchildren at every holiday, every birthday, every ballgame and, believe it or not, a few actually moved out of state to be near the precious creatures.

When my grandchildren came along, the first thing that hit me was the question of my longevity. Would I be around for their first day of school or when they walked down the aisle to get a diploma or get married? The math just didn't work.

It did not take long for the front of our refrigerator to fill up with snapshots. There are also pictures of the little darlings on the walls of every room of the house. It's as if we might forget what they looked like unless we were reminded as we walk from room to room. *Of course, at my age, that's a possibility!*

My wife is not the same person. Shopping for items for the grandchildren has been moved to the front of the prime directives. Logic and reason are gone. Grace saw a pair of shoes on television that she had to have. She claimed that she even dreamed about them. Grace's mother and grandmother went immediately to def-con 3. Grace must have these shoes. Stores were scoured, clerks were interrogated, and phone calls were made, e-bay was queried, the factory that made the shoes was contacted. All for Grace's well being. I would like to tell you that this campaign was a success, but no, the exact pair of shoes were never located. The mother and grandmother suffered from depression and failure for a while, but Grace graciously moved on to wanting a toy that had something to do with SpongeBob.

Once grandchildren are born, grandfathers lose whatever power we had or thought we had. We watch our wives take on a renewed purpose in life with the dedication that would embarrass a Marine. As for me, I have to say, I enjoy the kids. The older they get the more I enjoy them. But I like them in shorter interludes then my wife does. Let's say an hour at a time.

It didn't take me long to realize that no matter how many adults are in a room, if there's one child, the television is tuned on cartoons. Cartoons mesmerize the grandchildren. It's like giving them a drug. I never knew SpongeBob existed; now he's a familiar face.

Another awakening for me, was how many toys the modern small child must have to survive. Their rooms look like Toys-R-Us. With birthdays, special gifts and Santa, the inventory increases exponentially. I wonder if there are any toys left over for all the other kids.

My grandchildren are starting into school. A rite of passage has been reached. They have to take a test to get into the first grade. This exam is harder than some of my high school exams. The only thing I can help them with is to open the book and point to the page and say, "Read."

Do I recommend grandchildren? Sure, but watch out because you will never be the same.

STORIES ABOUT MY GRANDCHILDREN

If you aren't a grandparent, you may want to skip this story. Even those who do have grandchildren may get bored. If you make it all the way through, it is a testimony to your good manners.

WAKE UP CALL

I was sleeping soundly on my side of the king size bed; all of a sudden I became aware that someone was near. I opened my eyes and not two inches from my face was this little round face turned sideways to mirror my face. It was my granddaughter. She had this big happy smile as she said, "Papa, wake up."

TRUE WONDERMENT

We drove to Ocala, Florida, from St. Petersburg to pick up Grace and Ian from the other grandparents. Upon our arrival, Grace came running up excitedly to us as if the greatest thing in the world had just happened to them. She got right up in my face with her eyes wide with wonder as they looked into mine. She said loudly, "We had hot chocolate!, with marshmallows in it!"

Oh, to be a kid again, to experience for the first time the joy of hot chocolate with marshmallows.

CONDO CAPER

We were staying at a condo in Hilton Head, with Ian and Grace staying in a downstairs bedroom with Gigi, their grandmother. I woke up early in one of the upstairs bedrooms. I came out of the bedroom and stood on the second floor open walkway that connected the two upstairs bedrooms. I had a good view of the tiled entrance and the front door. The main floor bedroom was right off the entrance cove. Out popped this little head from the bedroom door. His face had the expression of, "look out world here I come." He had soundlessly escaped from Gigi's bed where he and Grace had been sleeping. They knew, that at their young age, they were not supposed to be out roaming around unattended but the curiosity of exploring had gotten the better of him. He looked outside through the side window panel next to the front door. Then he turned to view the living /dining room with an open cathedral ceiling and an open stairway that led upstairs to where I was standing. I could tell he felt free and he was on a big adventure that only the young and innocent can fully appreciate.

I made a small noise and he looked up and spotted me. His first reaction was to wonder if he was going to be in trouble. I smiled and waved for him to come up. He smiled back at me with a sense of relief and joy. Then he dashed up the stairs and we went into the bedroom, flopped on the bed and turned the television on to cartoons.

After about a half and hour of quality cartoon time together, his grandmother discovered he was gone. She came in like a storm, whisked him up and imprisoned him back in the downstairs bedroom.

Grandmother is not really the wicked witch of the condo; she is just concerned that they shouldn't be out exploring on their own at this age. She is just trying to teach the grandchildren between right and wrong. Grandfathers sometimes have trouble making that distinction.

FIRST BIRTHDAY

We had driven up from Florida to help Ian celebrate his first birthday. It was a huge affair that filled my daughter and her husband's house with well-wishers. Lisa, my daughter, loves to host large gatherings and this time she outdid herself.

While we were there, Ian learned to walk. It was a hoot. He was so glad that he finally could get from one place to another on his own. He would get up on his little wobbly legs and head for the kitchen where the cake and ice cream was. The only thing was that one of his legs would wobble too much and he would change direction without realizing it. He would keep going and end up in the dining room. He would look around; this wasn't the kitchen, so how did he get here? Then one of the guests interrupted his consternation by grabbing him up and showering him with attention. The kitchen, cake, and ice cream became a forgotten memory.

THE BIKE TRIP

When Ian was five years old I told him, "Ian when you are ten we will go on a long bicycle ride from Pittsburg to Washington D. C." As I was telling him he squirmed around and seemed preoccupied. After our brief exchange, he went on playing like nothing had happened.

The next day, Ian came up to me and said out of the blue, "Papa can we take the bike trip when I am nine?" "Sure," I replied, and he ran off to do whatever five-year-old boys do.

In analyzing his request, I wonder if he thought, five years is a lifetime. Four years sounds more doable. Or maybe he thought, *we better do the ride before Papa gets too old.*

PAPA GETS IN TOUBLE AGAIN

While riding home from church, Lisa informed Ian and Grace that their Sunday school teacher said that they had been little pills.
Lisa asked Grace, "Why did you act that way?"
Grace thought about it awhile and finally said, "The devil made me do it."
Lisa stopped the car because she hoped the Sunday school teacher had not said that. Lisa wanted to find out exactly where Grace had heard a statement like that.
"Who said that to you?" Lisa seriously inquired.
Grace quickly replied, "Papa."

A TRUE BELIEVER

At church, the teacher asked the children, "Who wants to be baptized?"
Ian raised his hand. The teacher asked, "Why do you want to be baptized?"
Ian answered, "So I can take God's hand and walk with him the rest of my life."
What an answer! The teacher was blown away. She then asked, "Who else wants to be baptized?"
Grace raised her hand, so the teacher asked her, "Why do you want to be baptized?"
Grace said, "So the other kids and I can jump in the water and play."
The teacher told Grace that maybe it would be better to wait a couple of years before making such a significant commitment.

A CHILD'S REQUEST

Ian came up to me one day and asked if Gigi and I would take him back to Florida?
I said, "Sure, what about Grace?"
Ian stated, "She will never find us."

AMAZING GRACE

I used to go around singing, *Amazing Grace*. One day Ian came up and said, "Sing Amazing Ian."

DISCIPLINE

One time we were taking Ian and Grace to Florida for a visit. Ian asked on the way down, "Do they have time out chairs in Florida?"
Gigi answered quickly, "They sure do."

A GRANDSON'S REQUEST

Ian, Grace and I were riding around in my little red convertible with the top down. A ride in the convertible is always fun. Ian turned to me and said, "Papa, when you get old and die, can I have this car?"
I would have been insulted by his request if he had not said first, *when you get old*. That's one of the cherished traits of innocent children; they say truthfully what they feel. Do we, as know it all adults, have that trait? I think not.

A RUN ON THE BEACH

When Ian was about four, we were swimming at the beach in South Carolina. With all his carefree nature, he was running down the beach just for the fun of it and the sheer joy of life. A boy his age came running the other way, mirroring Ian's emotions. Immediately and wordlessly Ian recognized a kindred spirit and quickly made a u-turn to run down the beach together. Oh, how quickly the young can make a friend. I'm envious.

THE MIDDLE THING

As our daughter picked up our six year old granddaughter, Grace, from her Sunday school class, the teacher informed Lisa that Grace had been very busy; getting into everything. On the way out to the car, Lisa proceeded to lecture the children on doing the right thing. She told them that they must learn to do the right thing, even if no one is looking. After listening to her mother's comment's about Grace's mischievous actions during class, Grace replied, "But Mother, I wasn't trying to do the wrong thing, *I was just trying to do the middle thing!*"

Upon hearing this story from our daughter, my thought was, "I think that's what happens to most of us, we all want to do our best, but most of the time we end up doing, *the middle thing.*

A DAY AT THE BEACH

The grandchildren are visiting so we are going to entertain them by a trip to the beach. They will enjoy it even though they live in Beaufort, South Carolina. Near them is Hunting Island, the most scenic beach I have ever seen. The palmetto trees cluster at the edge of the sand on the Atlantic Ocean. There is even a well-preserved lighthouse that adds to the atmosphere to this scenic shoreline.

But, anyway, we are going to take them to the beach in St. Petersburg on the sunny, sandy gulf. Both the grandchildren love the beach, so we will enjoy watching them have fun.

We start by packing our special beach chairs that have a canopy, which shields us from the ultra-violet rays of the sun. Other beach comforts packed include: beach towels, water bottles, snacks, suntan lotion, sun glasses, camera, books, sudoku puzzles, special beach shoes, buckets and toy shovels, and binoculars. It's a good thing we have a mini van.

In modern times, we try to keep the sand at bay. We don't want to lie in the sand or get the sand in our hair, shoes or the car. You might say the sand is our enemy.

I like to look out over the ocean with the white caps lapping up on the sandy shore and the white sea gulls flying to and fro emitting their shrill sounds. The smell in the air is of salt, fish and suntan lotion which floats in on a stiff sea breeze. The beach has a special sound and smell all its own.

In my youth, in the fifties, I thought the beach was the ultimate place to be. Growing up in Ohio with a very limited contact with beaches, my mind's visions were created by the movies where all the girls wore scanty swimsuits and a fun group gathered around a fire in the evening for hot dogs and frolicking.

In one movie, the great *Kahoona* lived on the beach in a shack built with driftwood and Moon Doggie and Sandra Dee hung out there with him. *Now that's a great life.* Sandra's perfect hair was never blown by the sea breezes and she never got sunburned. How lucky she was because in later years she might have had serious skin problems.

When I was a kid and read comic books, there was an advertisement on the back cover by *Charlie Atlas.* It started with him being a hundred pound weakling. At the beach, the bullies would kick sand on him and his girl. Since he was small, he didn't respond and his girl didn't think much of him. But then he sent away to *Charlie Atlas* and purchased this exercising program that made him big and strong. So back to the beach he goes with his babe in tow, and low and behold, the bullies are still there. They do the sand kicking routine again; this time he makes them pay for their dastardly deed. They end up running away. To his girl, he is a hero and all the people at the beach thank him for his heroics. Now he is the man of the hour and a real he-man who lived happily ever after.

I never ordered the life saving exercising program but I did fantasize about putting the bullies in their place.

When we come back from the beach with the grandchildren, we all take showers to get the sand out of our hair, clothes and teeth (if we snacked). The car has to be brushed to remove the sand and the beach towels have to be shook out and hung up. After all this is completed, we set back and reflect on a wonderful day at the beach.

FEBRUARY 7, 2011

Today was the day when I accomplished something really big in my life. It was not something that I had made a plan to do. It happened accidentally, which is the best way because it is a wonderful surprise. I am especially proud because I believe this catapults me up to the high echelon of senior *statehooddom*.

Today I took two naps. I arose before 7:00 am and after a busy morning of reading two newspapers, drinking four cups of coffee, doing two loads of laundry and finishing a hard sudoku puzzle, I lay back in my recliner. It was a little bit after noon. Well, you guessed it, I dropped off to sleep for my nap *numero uno.*

Then I woke up for the second time of the day, made a few phone calls, took a long walk and then had a lousy meal at the local Home Town Buffet. After returning to my humble abode, I decided to watch a tape of the 2010 Ohio State /Michigan football game. Even before the end of the first half, I was getting drowsy. I said to myself, *I can't sleep but I will go in and lie down on the bed and cover myself with my blue bathrobe.* And what do you know, I slipped off into another good sound refreshing nap.

When I woke up, it was raining hard like it can only do in tropical Florida. I snuggled under the bathrobe knowing that all was right with the world.

The point of this story is not to make the reader jealous, but just to convey the message of a day well spent.

THE NATIONAL DEBT

I have a plan for paying off the National debt: legalize marijuana. My plan is to let the federal and state prisoners grow and package the product for distribution. For their effort, the prisoners would receive one pack of twenty joints a week. These *dubies* would mellow out the inmates and render them less aggressive and more docile. Thusly, less prison personnel.

I would propose that the local police stations sell the product to the public. This way the police would know who the users are. They might even develop a non-adversarial relationship.

The selling and distribution of marijuana by the government would cut out the big drug cartels and the street pushers. The federal and state law enforcement would be freed up to hunt terrorists, rapists, and parking meter violators.

The prisons are now overcrowded with pot growers, sellers and users. My program reduces the prison population thereby saving the tax paying public huge amounts of money.

Those who are against legalizing marijuana say that the use of it leads to the hard stuff. My answer is, "Are all drinkers drunks?"

My conservative estimate is a billion dollar profit a year from selling pot. The federal government would get half of the money and the state and local governments the other half.

If my plan does not drastically reduce the national debt, then I propose a five percent reduction a year in foreign aid for the next ten years at which time the total reduction would be fifty percent. The small reduction would force all the foreign countries to adjust their economies appropriately.

If these two proposals still don't reduce the debt sufficiently, then I propose a closing of all military bases on foreign soil. We have had a military presence in Japan, Germany, Korea and England for the last sixty-five years. It is time for these countries to stand on their own. With our national debt being as high as it is, we should no longer try to support the economy of the world.

BANANAS ARE DRIVING ME BANANAS

I am trusted to buy very few items at the grocery store. After much coaching, sometimes I am allowed to purchase bananas.

I like big bananas and there is a tendency for me to lean towards buying big bananas when possible. My wife prefers small bananas and has certain reservations when I come blundering home with large bananas. To show her discontent she will eat half of the banana and then leave the other half, still in the peel, on the kitchen counter. It doesn't take long before that half of banana looks awful.

I have to choose bananas with some green on them but not too green and some yellow but not too yellow. There must be no brown spots on the bananas, ever! We only buy four or five bananas at a time so they don't get overly ripe and soft before their consumption. Who wants to eat a soft banana?

So now you are aware of the pressure that I stoically shoulder when sent to the store to buy bananas. That's not the last of it. I make my difficult choice on the bananas then I hurriedly bring them to the front of the grocery to check out before the bananas start getting too ripe. I can use the regular checkout person or check myself out in the fast lane. My time is precious to me. I didn't retire to wait in line at the grocery store.

The self checkout machine and I always have a dialogue. She, the voice in the machine, has no patience. The check out goes something like this:

"Thank you for using the self checkout machine."
"You're welcome."
"Have you scanned your Advantage Card?"
"No, not yet, give me a break, I only have two hands."
"Please place the scanned item in the bagging area."

"All right, I'm trying, where's the fire?"

"How do you want to pay?"

"Cash."

"That will be $1.31 please . . . . that will be $1.31 please."

"Yes, I'm trying to get two one dollar bills out of my billfold."

"Please take your change below. Please remove your items . . . . please remove your items."

"Thank you for using the self checkout."

"Hey lady, you're giving me a headache over five measly bananas."

POTPOURRI

BROKEN LEG

Many years ago I worked at Sun Valley, Idaho, a ski resort. Just in case you haven't been informed, skiing is hazardous to your health. You could break a leg. In fact, more than a few skiers did break their leg. So many, that those of us who worked at *The Valley*, became quasi-experts on broken legs. There is a fracture, a compound fracture, a spiral and a double spiral break. A double spiral break is the worst. It means that the leg is completely broken in two places and the bone could be sticking out through the skin. Nasty stuff. This type of break means you are laid up for nine months with crutches. So when we heard that one of our own broke his or her leg on the mountain, our immediate response was, "What kind of break is it?"

Well, after I returned to buckeye country, an acquaintance of mine broke his leg under mysterious circumstances. If I remember right, there was Burger Beer involved along with a motorcycle. This is a sinister duo.

I asked him, "What kind of broken leg do you have?" His angry reply was, "It's just a damn broken leg!" I thought about explaining to him my vast knowledge on broken legs but it would fall on closed ears. To him, he would always have just a "Damn broken leg."

My life's lesson learned here was that knowledge is sometimes compartmentalized into geographic locations. Sometimes it can be futile to intermingle knowledge from other regions.

WOMEN AT THE POKER TABLE

The popular belief by poker playing women is that the more cleavage shown at the poker table, the more distracted men will become. You know, I think they are right. I have seen a grown man leave a winning chair at one end of the table to take a seat at the other end of the poker table, just to be closer to the cleavage for a better look. Some men become mesmerized, like a deer caught in the headlights, at the sight of a slightly exposed woman's bust. Of course, I am unbothered by all this and my poker skills remain in tact.

A FELLOW TRAVELER

As an aging senior, sometimes you run into a contemporary you hardly knew from your youth, but now you smile and treat them like a long lost friend. These fellow travelers have made it through the challenges of life as you have, so you're glad to see someone from the past. They might not be perfect, but like you, they're still standing.

URBAN LEGEND

As an American adolescent male, I believed that girls were rendered defenseless by the strong masculine smell of men's cologne or after-shave lotion. As a hot-blooded youth, I would douse myself heavily before a date with the opposite sex.

I used Old Spice. It had an overly sweet smell, sort of like blooming flowers. We knew that girls adored the fragrance because the older boys said so and they knew everything about girls.

I can't speak for the other boys but I must have been using the wrong brand.

FOLDING CLOTHES

I believe that when women were young girls, they were secretly given instructions on folding clothes. They were taught how to fold them neatly and with no wrinkles. This uniquely women's talent puts men at a disadvantage for the rest of their lives.

CINCO DE MAYO

The reason that the Mexican holiday, *Cinco de Mayo*, is so popular in this country is because we, as a nation, like to say, "*Cinco de Mayo*." It has a nice ring to it. *Cinco de Mayo*, the phrase is almost like a rhyming poem, *Cinco de Mayo*.

I am told by people who should know the holiday, *Cinco de Mayo*, is not nearly as popular in Mexico as it is in North America. It is no big thing for Mexicans to say, "*The fifth of May.*"

THE THREE SECOND RULE

Until I had grandchildren I didn't know about the, "three second rule." It goes like this: if a morsel of food falls on the floor and does not stay there for over three seconds, it is acceptable to pick the bit of food up and eat it immediately without fear of contamination. Upon learning this new rule of life, I have accepted it whole heartedly and I haven't died yet.

ANNE WILLIAMS OWENS

On a cold rainy morning in May, in the 76th year of my life, a friend and I made a pilgrimage to the Radnor Cemetery at the uncivilized hour of 8:30 am.

My mission was to consult with my friend's nephew who is in charge of the cemetery and has access to the book that holds the graveyard burial sites.

I have been searching for my great-grandmother's grave for years. She has become an infatuation of mine and somehow I want to connect with her by knowing where she is buried.

She was born in Wales in 1843. Her name was Anne Williams. She married my great-grandfather, Thomas Owens, May 1, 1868, at the parish church, Vagnor, in the County of Becon.

Thomas Owens was born in Wales at Cefu Coed near Marlhyr Breconshire, South Wales, the 11th of November 1845. He came to America May 6th, 1863. The family story says that he was paid a bonus of $600.00 to enlist in the Civil War.

Thomas went back to Wales on March 2, 1868, to find a wife and after their marriage, they came back to America. They lived in Marion, Ohio. Anne presented Thomas with a son, Oliver Ivor Owens, on May 21, 1875. Oliver was my grandfather.

Anne died February 28, 1877. She was 34 years old. I feel sorry for her. She died young, away from her family and homeland. She passed away forty-three years before women got the right to vote. I surmise that her husband was dictatorial. He worked long hard hours smelting lime and came home tired and hungry.

After Anne died in 1877, Thomas went back to Wales in 1878 and married another Welsh woman named Rebecca Lewis. She lived until May 6, 1898. He married a third wife, Mrs. Clara Thomas. She later divorced him.

Thomas Owens is buried in Radnor Cemetery. He has one of the standard Civil War veteran grave markers. I have wondered for years where Thomas buried his first wife Anne.

Last winter, 2011, while in Florida, I received an e-mail from a wonderful, enthusiastic woman, from whom I had taken a genealogy course. She sent me two burial certificates from the Radnor Cemetery. One was for David Owens who died in 1870, and the other from Thomas Owens, who died in 1908. Connie, *Mrs. Genealogy*, projected that David Owens was Thomas' father. Both of these certificates listed the row and grave. (Row 33, grave 7 and 8)

So putting my super reasoning powers to work, I theorized that Thomas bought the gravesites in Radnor (five sites) in 1870 when his father died. He buried his father there in 1870. When his first wife, Anne, died, I believe that he, being a frugal man, buried Anne with his father. I believe that when his second wife, Rebecca, died, she was probably buried there also.

So if my count is right, there are four members of my family buried there; David, Thomas, Anne and Rebecca. The third wife sued him for divorce in December 1904; this was unheard of at that time. It was a messy divorce and I will spare you the ugly details.

I am satisfied that, this indeed, is where Anne Williams Owens is buried, in one of these five grave sites. My first cousins are visiting me for Memorial Day. Anne is their great-grandmother also. I want us to have a long talk with great-grandma. We will tell her about her nine grandchildren, what they were like and how they turned out in life. If we have time, we can bring her up to date on her eight great-grandchildren and what we went through to find her.

After our conversation, I believe that she won't feel alone in a foreign country anymore. She can finally be at rest knowing she has family here and is connected to them. I will have completed the journey and made the connection. The search is over.

This scenario sounds a little far out for a lot of people, but remember, we are of Welsh descent and cemeteries are a big thing in our lives.

GOUT

I read in the newspaper this morning that soda pop increases the chance of bringing on gout.

I have reoccurring gout which I am not especially proud of because gout is supposed to be and old person's malady.

My wife watches, *Doctor Oz*, every weekday. All the activity in the house comes to a halt. She records some of the good doctor's shows for future reference. She also has a pen and legal pad close to jot down some of the more poignant advice that must be remembered.

Anyway, Doctor Oz says that cherries help the pain of gout. So I have been placed on a regimen of a daily cherry pill. Well, to my surprise the cherry pill works. So now I must begrudgingly give Doctor Oz his just do. But I'm not going to watch him. If I listen to all those symptoms of disorders, I begin to imagine that I have all that stuff.

Being from Ohio, I have always called the fizzy stuff pop. In my travels to other parts of our country, I find that most citizens refer to the drink as soda. My grandchildren even call it soda. *What a country!*

Now that I am in my seventies, I wish to hide behind the old adage that, *something has to get me, why not pop.*

Some of the foods that have been blacklisted over the years by these *experts* have recently been found to have been unnecessarily demonized. The old experts must have died off. Now the new experts say, "Oh wait, butter, salt, sugar and red meat actually have some redeeming qualities that taken in moderation may be good for you."

I am not waiting twenty years for the atonement of pop.

CHURCH THEN AND NOW

There is an honorable group of people in our mobile home park in Florida that attend church on Saturday night. I don't think that going to church on Saturday night gives you full credit from above for weekly church attendance. To get full credit, the worshipper should attend Sunday services. Now, I know that some churches feel that Saturday is the holy day, well that's their business. To get full recognition for attending the church of your choice, you should not fall asleep during the sermon and it helps if your wife or lady friend wears a flowered or feathered hat. The real honor comes when you greet the minister at the church door as you leave. If you receive the double hand shake, your day is complete and the karma from a double hand shake is potent stuff. A double hand shake goes like this, you and the minister shake hands, then if the minister places his left hand on top of the handshake and you both smile and exchange some small talk, that's an A+ for attendance and you leave with the glow of virtue.

My daughter goes to a wonderful new, modern church. Everyone greets each other with smiles and they chat. There are no hymnals, because with new technology the words are projected onto a huge screen. A three piece music group dressed in jeans and T-shirts play all sorts of religious music that I am not familiar with.

The difference in dress code in churches from *my day* to now is overwhelming for us old-timers. In the old days a white shirt and tie was a must and the women wore their Sunday best. After all, the intent is to show respect for the Almighty, so you want to look your best. Not so now, anything is acceptable. I once saw a young lady in shorts. Shorts in church, what's this world coming to.

No baby's cry and scream in the new modern churches. The churches provide baby-sitting service for children of all ages. I ask you what kind of church service is it without a baby crying and an embarrassed mother or father carrying the precious child out in front of a grateful congregation.

In my youth, churches were not air conditioned. The windows and doors were open letting out the warm air but letting in all sorts of street sounds. To help keep the flock cool, there were little hand fans strategically placed in the pew by the hymnal. The worshippers waived these fans in front of their faces. Think of the dedication of the minister trying to get his sermon across over the fluttering fans and the traffic sounds from the open windows and doors. It's a wonder he could even preach at all.

Now, we have women preachers and my opinion to that is, "Why not!"

The one thing I miss most about the modern churches is that they don't sing the *Doxology*. You know, "Praise God from whom all blessing flow," and so on. I used to like to sing the *Doxology*. For one thing, I knew all the words and it meant the service was almost over. When we are away from home and our hosts ask if we want to go to church, I ask, "Is the service on Sunday and do they sing the Doxology?"

Even though so much has changed over time in the Sunday morning service, one axiom remains constant, people feel better about themselves after attending the church of their choice. So get out, go to church, but request the *Doxology* and a fan for old time's sake.

NIXON HAD IT RIGHT

We have just returned from an eight hundred mile trip to our daughter's, in South Carolina, for the holidays. For most of the trip we drove on inter-state highways. The natural flow of traffic on the inter-state highways now is between seventy and eighty miles and hour. The traffic also includes the big semi-tractor/trailers. These big trucks can legally carry up to 80,000 pounds. That's forty ton of metal cavorting down the highway at the speed limit or above the speed limit. This whole scenario seems more like a kamikaze event rather then a family outing.

To add to this cauldron of danger, is the dare-devil driver that wants to make it from Savannah to Jacksonville, which is about 150 miles, in an hour and a half. This driver shoots in and out of traffic with no regard to his or anyone else's safety.

The inter-state is also impeded by the driver doing the speed limit. The only problem is that he is in the left hand lane which is the passing lane. So our buddy that wants to *make time* has to pass on the right then whip back in front of our speed limit driver. The *make time driver* gives a long blast on his horn as he speeds on down the highway. Of course the guy in the left lane is clueless as to why he is being cut off and why in the world would they blow their horn at him. *He's doing the speed limit.*

If you remember back in the day, Nixon wanted us all to drive 55 miles an hour. You know, I think Nixon had it right. Think of all the fuel and lives that would have been saved in the last forty years, if the speed limit would have been 55 miles per hour. The economy would have been much better without these huge imports of oil. Think of how much cheaper it would be to produce a car that would cruise at 55 miles per hour rather than 75. My recommendation is to pass a law that would reduce car engines to a hundred horse power or less. Anyone having a bigger engine would have to pay a huge premium for tags and insurance. As for big trucks, I say 40,000 pounds is plenty big enough. That's twenty ton. Just think of the distance it would take a twenty ton truck to make a quick stop. Plus, the weight of the big trucks is what is breaking up all of our highways. The money we would save from having to rebuild our highways and inter-state system boggles the mind. If we had only listened to Nixon.

Nixon is not a good name to bring up these days as a person to admire. I am aware that he made some bad decisions. But you have to judge the man on his total career. Americans tend to evaluate a person whether good or bad on one deed. It's easier that way, you can just put him in the bad column and not have to think about him anymore. If he made one bad decision, he's out. We then decide that the man is worthless, and he never had a good idea in his whole life.

On a personal level, I don't think I have ever done bad-evil things but I wish I had been less selfish and more honorable. Sometimes in the night, the demons will come to remind me of all my regrets. Aunt Geneva told me once that things always seem worse in the night. Most mortals are good and bad and we only hope that when it comes to the time of judgment, there will be more good than bad.

This commentary has turned into quite a diatribe. I am not a Nixon man. I have been a life long democrat whose favorite president is Harry Truman. Let me end this commentary with a simple statement.

These United States would be a better place to live if we all slowed down to fifty-five miles an hour, Nixon certainly had it right.

LIFE WITHOUT TELEVISION

When we arrived home from Florida in April, we did a strange thing. We did not have the television cable reconnected. There is no live television in our condo. What percentage of American homes do not have television? I bet we are in the one percentile.

You say, "What on earth made you do a fool thing like that?" When in Florida, we had the top of the line dish cable—over two hundred channels to choose from. This is what every American family dreams of. In fact, all those channels are almost mandatory for those who want everything life has to offer. However, with all those channels, we ended up watching Andy Griffith or fifty-year-old reruns on the western channel. If I wanted to watch TV, I would channel surf through to see what was on. Forty-five minutes later, having gone through all the channels, I would decide there was nothing on that I wanted to watch.

We decided to leave the television off for the summer. We hoped to be traveling out west the last of August and the first part of September. Now, Ohio State lost its coach and quarterback, so why hook it up then? For my football fix, I can always impose on my dwindling set of friends to watch football on Saturday afternoons at their homes. However, being the *huge* fan that I am, I am feeling insecure just talking about not having the games available on my TV, so am sure that it will be turned on by football season!

By the way, we haven't renewed the newspaper either. The paper is getting smaller all the time and I breeze through it in ten minutes. I now gain my knowledge of current events by word of mouth. The only thing wrong with this is that everyone puts his or her own opinion or slant on repeating the news. One informed source told me, "That damn Obama served ice cream to some kids in the Rose Garden yesterday." I think there was a lot lost in the translation. For the weather, I have to read the skies like the Indians used to do. I haven't been right yet, but I am getting closer.

We can still play movies through our television. The library has many movies to choose from and they are FREE. I am in contact with the world through the internet. I am not sure if I completely trust the internet information. Who puts that stuff on there? If it's so up to date and accurate, why is it free?

We are about to complete our fourth month without America's favorite past time, television. Joyce has slipped a couple of times. She sneaked over to the neighbor's to watch *Dancing with the Stars*. As for me, my withdrawal shaking has subsided and some of my constant pacing has slowed down. I can now sleep through the night.

I would like to inform you of all the wonderful things I have accomplished in the time I have saved by not watching the boob tube, but, to my surprise nothing comes to mind. The only good thing I can say is,

"I haven't watched five thousand television commercials."

Update: The TV connection **was** reestablished just before the first OSU game was played!

THE CHECKERED FLAG

One of these days a doctor will look me in the eye and advise me that I am on my last lap. Some more tests will need to be run and some new experimental drug will be prescribed but basically the good doctor will be waiving the old checkered flag in my face.

Is this the time when I am supposed to wish that I had spent more time at the office?

No one can predict how they will react to the Checkered Flag. Maybe it's been a long race and they are tired. It could be an emotional relief that you finally know when the end will come.

As for me, I feel it was a privilege to have lived in my life's era: the freedom to run and play, unsupervised, as a child in the 1940s, my *Tom Sawyerish* existence in a small town, adventuring barefooted along the Olentangy River. These experiences cannot be duplicated in the present day. I am grateful for the experience of going to high school in the early 1950s, the innocents that was Delaware at that time, which was little affected by national and worldly events.

I can remember as a pre-schooler living on the farm with no running water or electric in the house. The changes that have taken place in the last seventy years are mind boggling; from those simple beginnings to a man walking on the moon, computers, jumbo jets, cell phones, television with 200 cable channels and an African-American in the White House. *Wow, is it any wonder we seniors suffer from dementia?* We don't have enough room in our minds to store all this newfangled information. My theory is that, when you get older your mind fills up so, when you learn something new something old is pushed out. We have no control over what is pushed out, it could be your cousin's husband's name or it could be where you put last years income tax form. All of a sudden, some things are just not up there anymore.

The old Checkered Flag is not a pleasant idea to contemplate but as a senior citizen we know that sooner or later it is going to wave for each of us. There's an old Chinese proverb that says, "May you live in interesting times." I think we have certainly done that.

MY OLD MAN

When you are a kid, your old man is your hero no matter how he acts, where he works or how he treats you. Dad was about five foot six inches and weighted one-hundred-thirty pounds soaking wet, as they say. He worked at the Ohio State Highway Department and he carried a black lunch box to work. When he came home, I always ran to meet him because he may have left just a little something in the lunch box for me.

Dad worked outside, resurfacing highways, on a truck that hauled tar and was called a distributor. The truck had an apparatus on it that heated the tar until it got very hot, then dad would drive the truck over the road and dispense the tar out the back through a spray bar. In the thirties, dad got blown off a distributor by an explosion of the volatile heated tar. He came home all wrapped in white bandages.

My father wore gray work pants and shirt to work. He probably bought them at the People's Store, which was a store where working people bought their heavy-duty work outfits. He also wore a dark hat with a round pin on it with a number, which confirmed that he was licensed by the State of Ohio to drive the big distributor. To me, as a kid, this outfit was comparable to an army general's uniform. It meant my dad was somebody and I was proud of him.

He worked with men who chewed tobacco and enjoyed each others' company. Men spitting tobacco juice was an action to behold for me. It showed that they were real men and I was in awe to be around them.

Sometimes dad had to make a trip to Circleville (50 miles away) or Washington Court House (even further away.) He would come by the house in the state pickup truck and I would get to ride with him. When I got back to the neighborhood, I proudly told my buddies where I had been; the day's trip was comparable to traveling to Paris, France.

Dad would set and read the paper and watch television at the same time. This was a feat that I could never quite do. He also would listen to the Ohio State football game on the radio and watch another game on the old black and white television. I could never do that, either.

We would ask Mom if we could go do this or that and she would say, "go ask your dad." He would never say, "yes." He always said, "I suppose so" or "I imagine." This used to bug me. Why didn't he say something like, "Sure you can, son."

Dad got me my first job on the summer crew at the Highway Department. We had to go down to the Democratic Chairman and he checked dad's voting record, then hired me. Dad and mom made many sacrifices on my behalf that I am grateful for to this day. The older I get the more I am impressed with the way I was raised and the patience they showed when I messed up.

Dad died at age fifty-eight on Friday the thirteenth in 1961. He had a huge funeral because he was very respected and he and mom came from big families.

When I think about my old man, many different thoughts run though my mind. I wish now that I had followed him around and learned to work on cars as he did, but I was busy running around having a good time. I never really understood my dad or his attitude toward life. I know that he loved me in his own way even though we didn't communicate much. I wish that I had been more aggressive in our relationship but maybe some things are not meant to be. I believe he tried and I tried but we were just not on the same page.

Dad must have had sinus trouble because he always hacked up and spit on his way up the front walk before he entered the house. I know that sounds gross but what I wouldn't give to hear him make that sound just one more time. He would come through the door in his gray work clothes with his lunch box. The smell of road tar would be clinging to him from his day's work. To this day, road tar is a pleasant smell to me because it reminds me of my old man.

WHAT TIME IS IT?

Before cell phones, when someone asked what time it was, the conversation went like this: One person would start by saying, "I just came by the big clock on City Hall and my watch was right on with the clock. The time is 11:58." Then the next guy would chirp in and say, "I set my watch by the radio this morning and it says 12:01." Another person would jump in with, "I have a Timex and, *it takes a licking and keeps on ticking,* and it keeps perfect time, it's 12:03." To keep the conversation going, another guy indignantly stammers, "I have my uncle's railroad watch and it's always right on. It's 11:55."

This animated conversation could go on for an hour. The talk was friendly and provided much enjoyment for the lack of anything else to converse about.

Since the advent of cell phones, these long lingering discussions about the time have come to a halt. One person will grab their cell phone, which is in constant contact with the official timekeeper, The Royal Observatory in Greenwich, London, England.

What a shame, now the conversation drifts back to the old stand by, the weather.

Don't get me wrong, cell phones are a great leap in technology. What would we do without our cell phones, maybe talk to the people around us?

Before long, we are going to have to explain to our grandchildren what a phone booth was, what it looked like and why it was needed.

My question is, who gave the Brit's the right to keep the big tally clock for the world? Google informed me that in 1884 during Chester A. Arthur's presidency, there was an International Meridian Conference in Washington D.C. to stabilize the time systems of the world. At that conference, the Greenwich mean time (GMT) was established. Now everybody in the world looks to Greenwich, England, for the exact time.

As for Chester A. Arthur, he became president on September 20, 1881, the day after President James Garfield died from a gunshot wound. After serving that term, he left office in 1885. Arthur was born in Vermont and was the son of a preacher.

Now, when some poor unfortunate person who doesn't own a watch or cell phone asks you, "What time is it?" Look them straight in the eye and say, "I set my watch by the sun dial that's in my back yard and the time is 12:00 noon exactly. You can bet the farm on it."

RON BON

This year, when I returned from Florida to Ohio, I discovered that one of my classmates from Willis High School had not made it through the winter.

Ron and I had not been close but we enjoyed conversing from time to time, every ten years or so. We had discovered that we had the same birthday, March 29. So each time we ran into each other, somewhere around Delaware, we would wish each other a happy birthday. It was our little joke and we both got a kick out of it each time.

Ron and I worked a summer together on the State Highway road crew. I called him Ron Bon, sort of my nick name for him. His name was Ron Bonnette. I remember one day in the summer, under a shady tree, during our lunch hour, three of us rowdy teenagers decided we would wrestle Ron to the ground. We couldn't do it. Ron was really strong.

Ron had this huge radio antenna on his house. One day he came to work and said he had listened to Columbus on the radio the evening before. I replied, "that's no big deal, I can listen to Columbus, Ohio, anytime I want." He said, "Columbus, Indiana," with a smirk.

I remember Ron always had this grin on his face, as though he had a secret joke and wondered if you caught it.

I used to run into Ron when he worked at Sears and Roe Buck on North Sandusky Street. After that, he worked at Delaware Appliance which was located next to the News Shop. I think I bought a stove from him when he worked there. Ron also worked at the Delaware Farmers' Exchange which was an old three story brick building on South Sandusky Street next to the railroad tracks. The railroad tracks are gone now and there is a new paved bike path where trains used to roam. This brick building had an old open cargo elevator. It looked just like the one you would see in the movies where someone has a loft apartment. Ron gave me a ride in the old elevator that we both thought was pretty cool.

I wrote a poem about attending old East School. A teacher there, Mrs. Smith, liked it and created a play using the words of the poem. She asked me over to address her fourth grade class and see the play. Ron was working maintenance for East School which is now called Conger. After wishing each other a happy birthday, we watched the play together. Our conversation was just as natural as if we were back on the road crew together.

Ron's and my last encounter was last year in Buehlers, the local super market. I was seated by the magazine rack, reading the magazines, free of course, when Ron walked up and wished me a happy birthday. After sixty years, I finally got around to asking him if he was born at Jane M. Case Hospital. He said yes but in questioning him further, I found that he was born in 1936 and I was born a year earlier in 1935. What a revelation.

Ron passed away this last January and I will miss not running into him any more. Too bad, I liked him and we went back a long way.

THE REAL ME

I like wearing blue jeans. I feel comfortable in blue jeans. In my youth, grade school and high school that's about all I wore. In school, we used to wear them so low that they barely clung to our skinny hips. *Weren't we something.*

I'm still wearing blue jeans. I'm not sure whether they are in or out of style, but who cares. Now I have to buy the relaxed fit. I guess that means I can relax better in them?

Sometimes to emulate my western heroes, I wear cowboy boots with my jeans. The boots add a little status to the outfit and they make a noticeable clomp when I walk. This alerts people of my presence.

I bought my first pair of boots in Idaho in the 1950s. They were light tan suede just like the folk singers were all wearing in that era. Ever since then, I have owned a pair of boots to accent my jeans and remind me of my early western days.

In 1972, I purchased a big green felt cowboy hat at a dude ranch in Colorado. I still have that hat and I cherish it. At Wall Drug, in South Dakota, in 1982, I bought a unique Indian band for my venerable old hat. The band adds a whole new style to the already perfect hat. The hat, band, boots and jeans blend perfectly together to make an outfit that makes a statement.

When we travel west, I wear this prized outfit everyday. It fits in perfectly out there in that beautiful, wide open country where cowboys used to roam. Most of the real cowboys are now gone but there are still many men and women who proudly wear jeans, boots and a western hat.

Last summer, in our trip west, my wife and I visited Deadwood, South Dakota. This scenic Black Hills country is steeped in spiritual Indian lore. Deadwood was where Wild Bill Hickok was shot while playing poker. He was reputed to have been holding aces and eights, which is now called, "dead man's hand."

Poker is one of my great joys in life. I'm not that good at playing but I love the game. I am reminded of a line in the movie, *From Here to Eternity*. Montgomery Clift was asked why he loved the army when they made him work sixteen hours kitchen duty everyday. He replied, "Just because you love a thing, it doesn't have to love you back." That's my sentiment about poker.

Back to Deadwood, where men are men and women are glad of it. Deadwood is now a legal gambling town with lots of casinos. I found a friendly Texas Hold'um poker game in one of the plusher casinos. I was dressed in my western outfit with the big hat. After setting in on the game for awhile, it didn't take me long to realize that the men at the table were all about my age and they were enjoying a leisure afternoon of friendly poker. I became aware from the banter around the table that the players were all from around the Deadwood area and had lived here for years. They were true westerners. None of them had a western hat on except me. During the pleasant flow of conversation, one of the men asked me where I was from. There I sat in my boots, jeans, and hat. What to say . . . what to say. I have always gone by the rule, if I can't come up with a good fib quick, revert to the truth. So I embarrassingly blurted out, "Ohio." The table became quiet, some players glanced down the table at me but the game went on. Now that I have had a chance to ponder a snappy reply, I should have said with a slow drawl, "Out Wyoming way, partner."

As I get older, I think I live more on the edge. I have been known to wear my western attire back here at home. I get some looks but there is usually nothing said. I figure if those gals in The Red Hat Society can get away with what they wear, why not me.

If you happen to see me decked out in my western outfit playing cowboy, don't say anything. This is who I am, the real me. I am relaxed and comfortable in my jeans, boots and hat and enjoying myself. *Isn't that what life is all about?*

CAPES

The other day, I was watching an Ohio State football game. The television camera zoomed in for a shot of Mr. Buckeye who was decked out in a white Ohio State outfit with a big ten-gallon western hat and get this, a white cape. I got to thinking, how long has it been since I have seen a cape?

My heroes, from the old comic books I read as a kid, all wore capes. You don't see capes anymore. Some men and women will throw their coats over their shoulders to make them look like a cape. Although this move has certain features of a cape, it falls short. A cape must be a cape. It must be worn with pride and dignity.

Superman, Batman, Robin, Captain Marvel, Superwoman and I think the Shadow all wore capes. It was a sign of status. Capes can be worn to help you fly, to wrap up in if you're cold, to hide your identity from the villains of the world and also to make a fashion statement like Mr. Buckeye.

Why have capes disappeared from our wardrobes? The world would be a better place if more capes were worn. Capes symbolize power, pizzazz and status.

I believe, as seniors, we should set an example for the young and uninformed members of our society and wear capes to bring them back to their rightful place of respect and to where they were when we followed our childhood heroes in the comic books of yesteryear.

JACOB AYERS

I was around sixty when I began to appreciate that I had a great-grandfather who was a scout in the Civil War. I had heard my mother and uncle tell the stories of his exploits but I was young and my reaction was, "great, what's for supper?" But then age caught up with me and I wished that I had listened a little closer to those colorful stories. Mom and Uncle Paul are gone now and I am here with no one to ask for details of his heroics.

Maybe I should start by telling the family stories as I remember them. Mom said that her grandfather had his horse shot from under him. He escaped and a southern belle literally hid him under her skirts from rebel soldiers. My great-grandfather stayed to help the woman get the crops in. Mom snickered with the inference that he may have stayed longer than needed.

My uncle's story was that my great-grandfather had his horse shot out from under him and he hid in some fallen timbers as the southern soldiers hunted for him. The rebels went back and forth looking for the yank. Finally, one of the *rebs* said, "I don't know where that son-of-a-bitch went. Lets get out of here." Years later, after the war, southern men came north to hire out to get the crops in. The women of the house would put on a big supper. Then after supper the men would move out on the porch to smoke, chew and talk. Usually the conversation would get around to the recent war. The men would tell stories of what battles they fought in and what part of the country they had traveled through. My great-grandfather recognized the voice of one of the men from the south. He then talked to the rebel about where he was located and when. Finally, great-grandfather said, "I was the son-of-a-bitch you were looking for." As the story goes, the confederate soldier was very apologetic.

My great-grandfather had fought at Gettysburg. He was assigned to the sixth army that came marching up from the south. His unit was one of the first to relieve Buford's Cavalry west of Gettysburg on the first day of the famous battle. After the war, any soldier that had fought at Gettysburg was respected and a hush formed when they told their stories of that pivotal battle.

One day, I was scrounging around the Delaware Historical Society research room looking for tidbits of information about Jacob Ayers when an acquaintance from Willis High School, who volunteered there, asked me who I was looking up. I told her Jacob Ayers. She left and came back with a file of letters. I couldn't believe what they were. I was dumb struck. There were letters that my great-grandfather had written home while he was in the Civil War. I am sure I was the first family member on my side of the family in three generations that knew of these letters. The letters were part of the "Sheets" family tree and had been in their family since the Civil War. The woman that collected them had transcribed them and typed them up so they were easier to read. The letters were all written phonically, such as, "I haven't rite in a wek." After reading all the letters, I couldn't spell any more. Of course, I'm not a star speller anyway.

Jacob Ayers's exploits were written up in the 1910 Delaware County History. He was personally interviewed and his accounts were fascinating. He was relating forty-six year old memories. My personal opinion is, that I am sure all those experiences happened to him but he had forty-six years to make them sound the best they could. He probably was a great story teller which he passed on to my Uncle Paul (Jacob's grandson) who kept me spellbound with his World War II adventures. In fact, this writer can spin a pretty good story if called on to do so. In the 1910 County History article, they called him Colonel Ayers. I am not sure how he attained this title. My guess is that he was one of the charter members of the Tannar Lodge of the Grand Army of the Republic. It could be that the GAR bestowed officer status on it's members. With all this said, he was still a respected person who fought in some crucial battles of the Civil War.

To be a good scout, you must have a daring attitude, sit a horse well and have a keen sense of direction in relation as to how you got where you are and how you plan to get back. In my small way, I have inherited a little of his direction in being able to figure out where I am on a trip and what direction to go to get where I want to be. I don't delude myself that I have his abilities. I only mention this because I feel deeply that we do inherit in our genes a lot of who we are both physically and mentally.

It's been 101 years since Jacob Ayers passed away and his great-grandson, who he never knew, is writing about him. His legacy lives on. In one hundred years, if I am lucky enough to have a great-grand child, I would hope that he or she might find a copy of this book so that my legacy would live on.

CEMETERIES

When I was a kid, we would go for an automobile ride on a summer evening or on a Sunday afternoon. Mom always wanted to go to the cemetery. I would rebel and say, "Mom, I don't want to go up and look at where people are buried." It didn't phase her. Dad would obediently drive the family up to the cemetery. Mom would then take over by giving us a tour of the family grave sites. She would say things like, "Now your grandfather is here and your grandmother is next to him. Your Aunt Myrtle is over there, she died young at thirty-three years old." This went on until she pointed to a vacant site and said, "Your Dad and I will spend eternity right there. When we get enough of the family up here, we'll play cards on Saturday night." When Mom told me about the card game, somehow that banished my squeamishness about cemeteries and dying. Mom took great comfort in knowing where she would spend eternity and with whom. Now, when my wife and I go for a ride, we always seem to end up at the cemetery.

In my opinion, it takes about three generations for grave viewers to stop dropping by to see you. There are some exceptions like genealogists or a snoopy great-grandson like myself.

If I was a good mathematician and could project population growth, it would not be hard to project when all our land will be taken up with cemeteries. Take Arlington National Cemetery for instance, in years to come, the cemetery could conceivably encircle Washington D.C. The United States would have to keep up it's war effort to accomplish this. But I am optimistic that our country can always find a war to get into somewhere on the planet and for some reason.

If cremation should become more fashionable, land would not be used up at such an alarming rate. Of course, if everyone had their ashes scattered in the oceans, then that would be another math problem as to when the oceans would be filled.

There is also a problem of marble for gravestones. What if the supply of marble runs short? One answer is that the marble could be recycled from old grave markers to new ones. Like I said, after three generations, who's to know. Use the emanate domain law if you have to. It works for new highways. The old marble stones could be photographed and recorded in the local courthouse for reference.

To tell you the truth, you can take my grave stone in a few generations. Once I'm in the ground, whether ashes or the other, I don't care. My major concern at that time will be shoveling coal or learning to play the harp.

With the way we are treating the planet, global warming; big holes in the atmosphere; reduction in farm lands; population growth and the National debt, I'm about ready to abandon ship. I think with a name like Gabriel, I might catch a break, upstairs.

After reviewing the above recommendations, I got to thinking. I have a great-grandfather who died in 1911 and I like to visit his grave and wonder what kind of a person he was. He was in the Civil War and fought at Gettysburg as a scout for the Ohio 82nd. I haven't started talking to him yet but I would miss his grave stone if it was removed. I am thankful to have a trace of his blood running through my body.

So far in these musings, it's been on my mother's side. On the Gabriel side of the family, I have a great, great, great (I think that's enough greats but I'm not sure) grandfather who was the first settler in Scioto Township in Delaware County. That is, he was the first after all the Indians who had been there for centuries. He was buried in 1815. I can take you to his grave and you can still read his grave stone after all these years.

After much contemplation, it may be better to leave the cemeteries the way they are. It has worked so far and as they say, "If it's not broken, don't fix it."

A CHANGE OF ATTITUDE

Do you get up in the morning and begin the same old routines? Is life getting boring? Let me tell you about what happened to me. My wife purchased a new coffee pot for me from Walgreens. It came in a neat box, which I slowly opened, to get the full pleasure of the new acquisition. Inside the box, was this beautiful, black and chrome coffee maker with a clear spotless carafe.

I put it together and I even read the instructions. This new shiny coffee maker really looks classy setting on the kitchen counter. The appearance of the whole kitchen has dramatically changed.

The new coffee maker has a clock and is programmable, so if I knew what time I was going to get up, my just brewed coffee would be waiting on me. I can even fill my cup while it is still brewing. It's like making a new friend.

When walking through the kitchen, I can't help but glance over at my stunning new appliance. It reminds me of when I was sixteen and got my first car, I would go to the window of our house just to look at my precious jalopy waiting for me at the curb.

Now, before I go to bed, I joyfully place the coffee and water in the new coffee maker and then when I arise the next morning I rush to the kitchen and push the button to start the brewing.

I go to bed with a whole new attitude of expectancy and I am ready to spring out of bed in the morning. If you want to change your life with a new attitude, buy a new coffee pot.

THE PERFECT AGE

When I was in my early teens, I thought that sixteen would be the perfect age. By that time I would know everything and be able to drive, which would let me cruise around town to see what's happening.

Then I became sixteen and the perfect age turned into twenty-one. At twenty-one, I would be out of school and not have the teachers and all those petty rules to follow. By law, I would then be a real adult and even have the right to vote. I could decide things on my own without parental direction. When I became twenty-one, I could drink anything alcoholic, legally, and not have to imbibe that rot-gut beer that was 3.2 percent alcohol. I know these are noble ambitions for a sixteen year old but what can I say?

It seemed like overnight that I arrived at the ripe old age of twenty-one. I soon found out that twenty-one was not as perfect as I thought it would be. I was supposed to be an adult but I found that to my dismay, I did not know everything. My mind roosted on the idea of age and when would I be old. Well, at twenty-one, thirty seemed old. Dad and mom were off the charts. Would you believe they were around fifty. *Now that's really old.*

Time goes by quickly and I zoomed through my twenties, thirties and forties. Before I knew it, I was fifty. I decided my parents must have aged poorly because I was now fifty and I didn't feel old, so I decided old was now sixty-five.

It wasn't long until sixty-five rolled around and I still didn't think I was old. So what age is old? A perplexing question. After much thought and observing the old timers I knew, I placed old at eighty. By this time, I was tired of recalculating what was supposed to be old.

Now, I am rushing through my seventies and will hopefully reach eighty soon. My thinking of eighty as old has not changed. In fact, my thinking now, is being old is respectable and honorable. It is a noble accomplishment and if I am fortunate enough to arrive at that pinnacle with all my faculties, I promise not to ever worry about old age again. Eighty, in life's journey, is my next goal.

You know, I think I might have missed the boat on this age fixation; now I think the key is to enjoy each age as you live it. I remember saying to dad, "I wish it was summer," or "I wish Christmas would get here." He would always admonish me with, "Son, you're wishing your life away." Well dad, you were right, but it's too late now or as the Amish say, "Too soon old, too late smart."

MY DEAREST DAUGHTER, LISA

I can't bring these ramblings to a close without mentioning your place in the memories of my life.

When you were young, and your mother worked at the phone company in the evenings, you and I were on our own. It was never a bother to baby sit you because I always enjoyed being around you. I remember you and I riding down to the phone company with your mother. We would stroll back home together. The West School playground was on the way so we would stop and you would play on the equipment there. If there were any other children there, you would walk right up and start playing with them. Before long you would be one of the group.

Saturday mornings was our time. We would jump in the little, green Volkswagen and head out. We usually went to visit the grandmothers but sometimes we dropped in on aunts and friends. I remember about truthfully answering your question about Santa Claus on one of our Saturday morning rides. The next question out of your mouth had to do with the Easter Bunny. Of course, I had to be truthful with that question too. *Wow, what a day in your young life, to find out about Santa Claus and the Easter Bunny within ten minutes.* You never asked me about boys, you must have figured that one out on your own.

It seemed to me that each age you were, was the best. I wanted to stop you from getting any older because I loved you just the way you were.

Then you became a teenager. What a happy, busy girl you were. I remember teaching you to drive. It didn't take long because you wanted wheels in a big way. After that, it seemed that you were always out and about, driving a stick-shift Chevy pickup to school and around town. That was cool. At that age, you ate so much pizza that I thought you were going to turn into one.

Your mother and I have followed you around the country, to New York City, Seattle and Beaufort, South Carolina, which has given us many fond travel memories.

Then it happened, after we had almost given up the idea of grandchildren, you presented us with two active, ornery, wonderful grandchildren. The grandchildren have renewed our vigor for life. Your mother can't go shopping now without purchasing something that the dear grandchildren need. Of course, she always saves me money because she got the item on clearance or on a special sale.

You have settled into a very busy daily schedule. This is why your old man can only stay plugged in for a limited time. Your happy, active, action filled days are way above my tolerance level. I am at the age where I need peace and quiet to endure with some semblance of sanity. But I still love you, your family, your two dogs, your three guinea pigs and the various neighborhood kids that are lurking about. It's just that I find it less nerve wracking to love it all from afar, like 700 miles.

You have developed two virtuous traits, that are admirable. One is your determination and the other is how hard you work to get life the way you want it. You have determined that you are going to provide your children with as many wonderful experiences in life as you possibly can. You are also putting your total effort into each day to try to give your family a good life. Also, you always place everyone else's needs above your own.

You have an open-house hospitality for everyone, which reminds me of my mother and the home I grew up in. I hope your children bring you as much happiness as you have brought your mother and I.

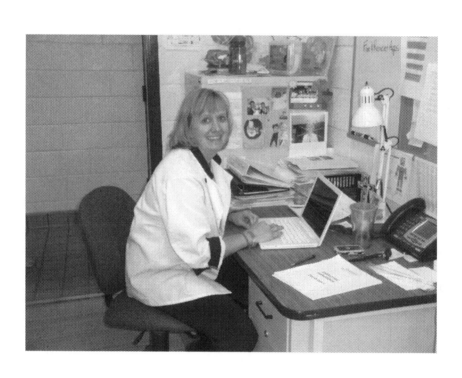

MOM

In these stories of my life, there has been references about my mother. She has been the greatest influence in my life. She loved me unconditionally, which meant she overlooked all my many shortcomings.

Mom liked people and they liked her. She had an open home where friends, family and acquaintances dropped in, unannounced, anytime. They were always welcome and never had to worry that they were interrupting her schedule. She entertained, with what seemed like effortless ease that relaxed her guests. Her hospitality and delicious meals were enjoyed by all.

She was a very giving person and it made her happy to make other people happy. She has been gone for thirty-six years and I am still getting comments on her many good deeds.

My mother's idiosyncrasies were many and I remember them with loving humor. She was superstitious to a fault. If a knife dropped on the floor, it meant that company was coming from the direction the knife was pointing. I was scolded many times for laying on the floor while watching television, and rocking the empty rocking chair with my foot. It had to do with spirits. Of course, the more I was scolded the more I tried to get away with the ghostly rocking.

My aunts and mother, when visiting someone else's house, would have to leave by the same door they entered. It had something to do with leaving your spirit in that house. I say it's a poor spirit that can't follow you out a different door. Having said that, I must confess to sometimes making a special point of leaving by the same door I entered. Who's to say that mom and her sisters were wrong? *Not me.*

Mom was afraid of thunderstorms. She would sit in the stairway with her fingers in her ears and her eyes closed. Plugging in the electric iron was another fear of mom's. She would have my sister or I plug the iron in. I guess she felt that we were immune to being electrocuted.

I never knew mom to read a book. The only thing that mom read in the newspaper was the horoscope and *Dear Abby*. Clark Gable was her heartthrob, but she named me after Ronald Coleman, who was a movie star in the 1930s. I have always wondered if she named my sister, Sally, after the famous fan dancer, Sally Rand.

I have inherited my mother's gift of gab. My wife informs me that I can carry a twenty minute conversation with a wall.

When you truly respect a person, you trust their actions and opinions. They become your heroes. When I am faced with a dilemma or a hard decision, I try to imagine how mom would have handled the situation.

My mother deserves and has my total gratitude and admiration for the examples she set for me. I feel very fortunate to have had her for a mother.

NOW-A-DAYS

For the last ten years, Joyce and I have wintered in Florida. The term used by those in the know is, *Snow birds*. Our schedule is six months in Florida and six months in Ohio.

It's a good life and I am grateful for it. Back in the fifties, I had an aunt and uncle who migrated to Florida in the winter. At that time only the well-to-do could stay in Florida for the winter. Now, here I am, but I believe I am more lucky than rich.

In Florida, we live in a resident-owned mobile home park. The park was built in 1966. It is laid out in circles. The clubhouse, swimming pool and shuffleboard court are in the center.

The residents come from many different states and Canada. The Canadians chide us because we know nothing about their country. They had to learn all our states and capital cities in school. We don't even know the location of their providences, let alone the capitol cities of those providences.

In our park there are 123 units (never say trailers). All those who migrate down for the winter leave their family and friends for the benefit of warm weather and sunny blue skies. They are in the mode of reaching out to find new friends and acquaintances. The park has many social functions so that the residents can meet and get to know each other.

For me, there is poker on Monday night, euchre on Tuesday night, and bingo on Wednesday night (I call the numbers,) to keep myself occupied. There is also shuffleboard on Tuesday and Thursday mornings, bike riding, walking, shopping, eating out and two hundred channels of television to fill the vacant time between activities.

There is a bike trail close to the park that goes from downtown St. Petersburg up to Tarpon Springs. This Rails to Trails paved path runs about 45 miles.

I would feel very isolated if I lived in a regular single-family residence down here.

This last season we had two of my life long friends and their wives down for a week. One couple came in February and the other in late March. It is a great joy to have old friends. If you have a special contact that lasts for sixty years, you must be doing something right. This year I told Don's wife, Eleanor, that if someone phoned and told me Don had killed somebody, my first reaction would be that somebody must have needed killing. Friendships deepen with age. Jobs, raising children and life's obligations get in the way during the middle years. But in retirement the friendships have time to blossom.

Our daughter, Lisa, lives in Beaufort, South Carolina. Beaufort is an old southern town with large antebellum homes and tall oak trees with huge limbs growing out horizontally. The road from Ohio to

Florida goes right through Beaufort. We also spend Thanksgiving and Christmas with Lisa, her husband, Steve, two children, Ian and Grace, cat (Allycat,) dog (Mimi,) dog (Dulley,) Guinea pig (Fidget,) and Lisa's in-laws from Wisconsin, Fran and Mary Lou Eklund. Joyce visits Lisa in late January for two weeks. Lisa's birthday is January 30th, and Ian's birthday is February 3rd. Then in June, Joyce, spends two more weeks in Beaufort for Grace's birthday.

While in Delaware, I go back to my tried and true noble endeavors of card playing, Ohio State Football, genealogy, talking old times with old friends, of course, and writing these stories.

One great addition to our lives, as we live it now, is the cell phone. Everyone seems to have a cell phone with lots and lots of free minutes. This provides us with the opportunity to stay much closer to our friends and family by phoning them often with no expensive phone bills.

So, you can see that life is good and has become a pleasurable routine of holidays in Beaufort, winters in Florida and the reconnecting with old friends and familiar surroundings in Delaware.

As I speed along through my seventies, I have no idea what twists and turns life has in store. Life can change very quickly at my age. I am grateful for my reasonably good health and an exceedingly full, active retirement. Each day is taken as a gift and I am hoping for a busy happy future.

Happy trails to you.

Ron and his wife, Joyce, live in Delaware, Ohio. They are retired and spend their winters in Florida. This is Ron's first book. He has been writing these stories of his life for over ten years. Ron does the writing and his wife is the editor and consultant.